The Ultimate Guide to Homeownership in Jamaica

Claudia Davis

Published by Claudia Davis, 2024.

While every precaution has been taken in the preparation of this book, the publisher assumes no responsibility for errors or omissions, or for damages resulting from the use of the information contained herein.

THE ULTIMATE GUIDE TO HOMEOWNERSHIP IN JAMAICA

First edition. October 16, 2024.

Copyright © 2024 Claudia Davis.

ISBN: 979-8227311566

Written by Claudia Davis.

Table of Contents

First, I give thanks to the Creator for guiding me through this journey and for the many blessings along the way. To the countless individuals who have shared their wisdom, inspired me, and provided guidance throughout my life—this book would not have been possible without you.

To my dear children, Rachel and Toni, and my cherished grandchildren, Xander and Xaven—this book is for you. May it be a guide on your path to homeownership and financial success. I hope the lessons and stories within inspire you to build the future you deserve, with strength, determination, and faith.

With all my love,Claudia

PREFACE

"From Trials to Tiles: My Journey to Homeownership"

The morning sun of July 1982 brought with it a harsh awakening as I found myself lying on the floor. Gradually, the foggy remnants of the previous day's events began to sharpen into painful clarity, each memory striking with the force of a wave, relentlessly flooding my mind with tears that I struggled to hold back

Saturdays had always been our days for adventure—my cousin and I reveling in youthful laughter and carefree trips to the plaza. At 16, she was exploring romance with her Rastafarian boyfriend who lived nearby, while I, a year younger, had yet to experience such things. Our routine was simple: a visit to see him, some time spent hanging out, and then home. However, this particular Saturday veered off course, reshaping my life in ways I hadn't anticipated.

We didn't come home to the warmth we expected, but instead were met with harsh accusations from my aunt, supported by my dad's stern look. Their message was clear: if we were old enough to seek adult freedoms, we were old enough to face adult responsibilities. They told us to leave. Stunned, I packed a few essentials—clothes, books—and with my cousin by my side, I walked into a future filled with uncertainty. I vowed never to look back or return.

As we walked away, my heart was heavy yet somehow also lightened. I felt a strange sense of relief. The past three years living there had been difficult, ever since my other cousin rescued my brother and I from a challenging life in Jones Town, where our mother had left us with a promise that "Your father will come for you." What was supposed to be a day turned into three long months until our rescue, now, facing abandonment once again. The next morning, I awoke in a cramped, single-room at the back of a house, rented by her boyfriend—a space too small to comfortably accommodate the three of us. Recognizing we were intruders in this temporary refuge, I sensed it was only a matter of time before we would need to move on. Thus began a period of couch-surfing, relying on the generosity of friends and neighbors who offered me places to sleep. Despite their kindness, I felt the instability of my situation keenly and reached out to my mother in the US, hoping she could offer a solution. Eventually, she directed me to Waterhouse, where I could stay with the sister of my half-brother.

In that neighborhood, marked by frequent gunfire, I found another temporary place to stay, sharing it with someone else living transiently. Amid the chaos, I knew this place wasn't my final stop. School remained my only stable factor, grounding me amidst the turmoil. During this time, my cousin—the one who had rescued me from Jones Town—returned into my life, offering a haven with Aunt Dolly. Aunt Dolly's home was a sanctuary of warmth and support, providing not just a physical space but also emotional comfort.

Beneath Aunt Dolly's comforting roof, as I diligently prepared for my Fifth Form exams, the precariousness of my situation became starkly apparent. Aunt Dolly, in her twilight years, provided a stable sanctuary, yet the troubling thought persisted: what would happen when she could no longer offer me shelter? Amidst this uncertainty, a firm resolve formed within me—I needed my own house, a place where I could lay down permanent roots and choose my own bed.

Despite the upheavals of my youth, I succeeded in passing five subjects in my exams. However, life was about to take another unexpected turn. At 17, I discovered I was pregnant, a revelation that overwhelmed me with fear and uncertainty. But Aunt Dolly's resilience steadied me. "Stop the crying," she insisted. "You're not sick. You'll have your baby, go back to school, work, and care for your child." Her encouraging words and steadfast support helped me weather the emotional storm of impending motherhood.

My mother, although far away, remained a crucial support, regularly sending barrels of clothes and food that sustained me and my young daughter. I took on various odd jobs that matched my skills until a friend's attempt to join the army inspired me to do the same. We both failed initially; she moved abroad, but I persisted and eventually succeeded. My service in the army, including training at New Castle and the Royal Military Academy Sandhurst, England, honed my resilience, instilling in me discipline, endurance, and a profound sense of leadership.

After my military service, a twist of fate led my daughter and I back to the very house I first sought refuge in after being expelled by my father. A friend pat helped me secure a position working in a mailroom at an Insurance Company.This allowed me to rent a single room, sharing common facilities. The irony of returning to that starting point underscored my resolve to change my circumstances. It was during this period that I came across "The Richest Man in Babylon," a book that echoed and fortified my own aspirations of homeownership. By the age of 23, I had achieved that dream—I became a homeowner and was working as a Telephone Operator. With my daughter by my side, I moved into our house, a place that was truly and entirely our own.

I owe my achievements not just to my own efforts but to the unwavering support of family, friends, colleagues, and acquaintances who've guided me throughout my life. Central to this support network was my mother, who instilled in me a love for reading. She fueled this passion by purchasing books every Friday from downtown Kingston and having me read aloud to her each evening after work. This practice not only honed my reading skills but also provided me with invaluable knowledge that has been crucial in all my endeavors. Even after she relocated overseas when I was 12, her commitment never wavered. She consistently sent barrels filled with food, clothes, toys, and cosmetics, ensuring we had the resources we needed and showing her enduring support from afar.

My father was my earliest mentor in mental arithmetic, hustling, and salesmanship. Growing up around the bustling markets of Spanish Town Road, Falmouth, and Savanna-la-Mar, and his thriving BAR. He taught me to check stock and make change mentally with no calculator or book and pencil. Those were invaluable mental abilities and sales techniques that later propelled my entrepreneurial endeavors. Although he made the decision to have me leave home at age 15, the lessons he taught me were crucial as I navigated my own paths in hustling and eventually in real estate sales. This challenging moment underscored the importance of self-reliance and pursuing my ambitions, instilling in me a firm resolve to own my home and the principle of relentlessly moving forward. It taught me the importance of focusing on the present, dreaming big, and working diligently towards a future shaped by my own aspirations. After all, I am the only one who can dream, desire, and build my life—no one else can do it for me.

I must also talk about my Aunt Dolly who was a beacon of stability, always there to take care of my daughter when I still wanted to party, teaching me the ropes of rent collection and the importance of living within our means until we could afford to reach higher. Her wise words "Claudia better you walk if nutting dan sit waiting for something" still ring true to this day. Her wisdom taught me the value of taking action, even if it means walking without a clear destination, rather than passively waiting for something to happen. Her wisdom still rings true today, as I continue to navigate numerous Real Estate deals and sales that come my way, often while driving around without a clear destination in mind.

This lesson also became evident when one of these walks in my neighborhood led me to meet Nigel and Hanson, my teenage supportive neighbours. They allowed me to be a teenager navigating parties and the like, looking back what fun times we had, but better yet they handed me forms to sign up for the HEART school leavers program. They and their families, too, became pillars of strength when I found myself navigating the challenges of teenage motherhood.

I must talk about and say special thanks to my high school friends, both named Jacqueline, who offered their homes as sanctuaries of stability and warmth during my tumultuous teenage years. I would often hang out at their house and one helped me washed and styled my hair on saturdays and introduced me to a skin care product line Jencare which I still use to this day. The other taught me Maths and Physics and encouraged me to venture into the army, setting me on a transformative path that built a foundation of strength, honour and loyalty within me.

In my professional life, friends and colleagues have also played crucial roles. I must say special thanks to Pat who not only helped me secure a stable job but also encouraged me to buy my first home when I faced a sudden rent increase and guiding me through the complex sale agreement. At work, my colleague Richard and my boss Mr. Squire directed me towards a housing scheme that became my first property investment, offering invaluable advice at critical moments. Also Richard's sister Juliet, who lived in the same scheme, gave me and my young daughter lifts in her VW Bug to school and work . Her warmth and kindness inspired me to invest in my own 1970 VW Bug.

Another Richard, whom I call my godfather was instrumental, offering essential support by cosigning my loan for my first home, he was right there when I needed it most. His actions revealed to me the presence of a greater guiding force, a power so immense that it can make the impossible achievable. All it takes is that initial step, and the universe will orchestrate divine intervention precisely when we require it.

I must also acknowledge and say special thanks to the fathers of my two daughters, whose varied emotional, educational and financial support paved the way for many of my successes. They embedded within me the essence of what unconditional love looks and feels like, free from any conditions or expectations. As a woman, they empowered me to take bold steps, like when I walked off my job! wow what a bold step that was, but their presence gave me surety that if I ever stumble or falter, they will be there to ensure my landing was soft and gentle.

And of course, my daughters, Toni-Ann (named by my friend Jacqueline) and Rachel (named by her dad) have been constant pillars of support and inspiration through every challenge and triumph. Their commitment to our unity as a family, living and working together to pursue both shared and personal aspirations, has brought me immeasurable joy. I feel like the happiest mother ever created by the universe.

Last but certainly not least, my two grandsons, Xander and Xaven, alongside their dad Brent, who both came into this world amid a pandemic, have sparked in me the determination to begin documenting my journey. It's important to me that they grasp the depth of the remarkable family they were born into and have embraced.

Reflecting on my life, I see how crucial each of these relationships has been. This network of support was not just beneficial; it was essential to my successes. Thus, I encourage you to build your own support network, whether it's friends, family, mentors, coaches or partners. Seek out those who will stand by you, inspire you, and help you to navigate through challenges. Most importantly, remember to read financial and motivational books so that you can gain the knowledge of the people before us. Therefore, I recommend the following books:

"The Richest Man in Babylon" by George S. Clason, this book will start you on the teachings of financial education and how to be wise with your earnings, which is fundamental to your success

"Think and Grow Rich" by Napoleon Hill which highlights the value of mastermind groups. These groups can significantly amplify your potential and help you achieve more than you might initially believe possible. Being part of a supportive community not only increases your likelihood of success and eases your burdens but also enhances your journey with shared experiences and collective wisdom.

With that being said, I hope you have your own reasons and a burning desire to own your own home so here's to celebrating your success!

CHAPTER 1

The Journey Begins: Lessons in Homeownership

My awakening and introduction to the significance of a home began at the tender age of 15, on the day I was abruptly told to leave the house where I lived with my father with nowhere else to go. That jarring moment underscored a basic human need for shelter—a place to call one's own. After bouncing around at various places I eventually went to live with my Aunt Dolly, in Kencot,she offered me a home and showed me a new lens on homeownership.

A migrant to England in the '50s, she had envisioned returning to a home in Havendale, only to find that her hard-earned money had been spent on a house in Kencot—a neighborhood less prestigious, a "ghetto house," as she put it.

Aunt Dolly's initial distress over the location slowly transformed into determination. The house, a duplex, became both her home and a source of income; she chose to rent out half while residing in the other. It wasn't just a structure but a living, breathing investment that housed generations—Nanna and Pappa, her two adopted children, her elderly mother, myself, and eventually, my own baby. With every rent collection round, I absorbed the intricacies of being a landlord, witnessing firsthand the potential of property to yield financial returns.

This resilience is emblematic of many Jamaicans who, like Aunt Dolly, can turn 'lemons into lemonade.' It's a quality mirrored in the Jamaican real estate market, as vibrant and resourceful as the island's populace. Jamaica presents a tapestry of real estate options: from the promise of plots waiting for the stamp of new homes to serene beachfront villas, the energetic hum of urban apartments, and tranquil rural retreats. The market's rhythm is dictated by diverse forces—the allure of tourism, the homeland call to the diaspora, and the steady march of local economic growth and infrastructure advancements.

As prospective homeowners and investors look to Jamaica, they find a market rich with opportunity and steeped in a history of overcoming, adapting, and flourishing. Here, the dream of homeownership is alive and well, rooted in the belief that real estate is not merely an investment in land, blocks and steel but a testament to the enduring spirit of its people.

Current State of Real Estate in Jamaica

The Jamaican real estate market has recently experienced strong demand for residential properties, driven by both local and international buyers. This surge is supported by a growing economy, enhanced infrastructure, and a thriving tourism sector that continues to draw visitors and investors. Property prices vary significantly across different parishes, with prime locations like St Andrew, St Ann, St James, and the north coast commanding higher values due to their popularity and ongoing development.

Also, the Jamaican real estate scene is experiencing growth with numerous new projects, such as gated communities, apartment complexes, and luxury estates. These developments cater to diverse preferences and feature modern amenities, robust security, and options for sustainable living, aligning with international housing trends.

The real estate market in Jamaica presents numerous opportunities, supported by policies that favor both local and international investors. However, navigating this market requires careful planning, informed decisions, and an understanding of Jamaica's legal, economic, and cultural context. With proper guidance and preparation, purchasing property in Jamaica can be a fruitful investment and a doorway to the country's dynamic and picturesque lifestyle.

The Jamaican real estate market offers a wealth of opportunities, backed by a Legal framework that supports both local and international buyers. However, the unique aspects of the market demand careful navigation, informed decision-making, and an appreciation of the island's legal, economic, and cultural nuances. With the right preparation and guidance, buying a home in Jamaica can be a rewarding investment and a gateway to experiencing the rich, vibrant lifestyle of this beautiful island.

CHAPTER 2

The local laws and regulations governing property transactions

Navigating the real estate market in Jamaica requires an understanding of the local laws and regulations governing property transactions. These legal frameworks are designed to protect both buyers and sellers, ensuring transparency and fairness throughout the process. For anyone considering buying a home in Jamaica, familiarizing yourself with these key legal considerations and the role of government and agencies is crucial.

Legal Framework and Ownership Rights

Jamaica operates under a system of "Common Law," which provides secure ownership rights to property buyers. However, the process of transferring property ownership (conveyancing) can be more complex and time-consuming than in some other countries, emphasizing the need for reliable legal advice and due diligence.

Land Registration: The Jamaican government has implemented a system of land registration that provides buyers with a title guarantee. However, there are still properties, especially in rural areas, that are not registered. Buying unregistered land can pose risks and complications, so it's crucial to ensure that the property purchase includes a clear and registered title.

Key Legal Considerations for Home Buyers

Title Registration and Searches: One of the first steps in the home-buying process is conducting a title search to verify the seller's ownership and ensure the property is free of any encumbrances, liens, or disputes. Jamaica's system of land registration provides a reliable record of land ownership through the Registrar of Titles. Buyers must ensure that the property they intend to purchase has a registered title, as this simplifies future transactions and enhances the security of your investment.

Stamp Duty and Transfer Tax: Property transactions in Jamaica are subject to stamp duty and transfer tax. Stamp duty can be shared equally between the buyer and the seller or negotiated as to which party pays, while the transfer tax is typically the seller's responsibility. However, the allocation of these costs can be negotiated as part of the sale agreement.

Sale Agreement and Conveyancing: The sale agreement is a crucial document outlining the terms of the property sale, including the purchase price, deposit amount, and completion date. After signing the agreement, the conveyancing process begins. This involves the legal transfer of property ownership from the seller to the buyer and usually requires the services of a lawyer to ensure accuracy and compliance with Jamaican law.

Market Accessibility for Overseas Buyers: Jamaica is relatively open to foreign buyers, with no significant restrictions on property ownership by non-residents. However, all buyers including foreign buyers must apply for a Tax Registration Number (TRN). Here is the link [on how to apply for a TRN.](https://www.jamaicatax.gov.jm/trn.html)

Mortgages and Financing: For buyers requiring financing, understanding the mortgage process and requirements in Jamaica is essential. The National Housing Trust (NHT), banks, credit unions, and building societies offer mortgage products, each with its criteria, interest rates, and repayment terms. Foreign buyers should note that financing options may vary and sometimes involve additional requirements.

Cultural Considerations: The process of buying a home in Jamaica can be influenced by local customs and negotiation practices. Building relationships and understanding local market dynamics can be as important as the financial and legal aspects of the purchase.

The Role of Government Agencies in the Home-Buying Process

Several government agencies play a pivotal role in the Jamaican home-buying process, ensuring compliance, facilitating transactions, and offering support to buyers:

Registrar of Titles: Operates under the Land Registration Act, maintaining land titles and ensuring the accuracy of land registration and records. This agency is vital for conducting title searches and registering new ownership after a sale.

National Land Agency (NLA): The NLA is responsible for land administration and management, including surveying, mapping, and registration services. They provide essential information for property transactions and development.

National Housing Trust (NHT): The NHT offers financing options for Jamaican citizens, including loans for purchasing, building, or repairing homes. It plays a significant role in making homeownership accessible to a broader segment of the population.

Tax Administration Jamaica (TAJ): The TAJ is involved in the assessment of stamp duty and transfer tax associated with property transactions. This section is called Stamp Duty and Transfer Tax and is a division of Tax Administration Jamaica (TAJ). This office is responsible for the assessment and collection of stamp duty and transfer tax related to property transactions. Stamp duty is a tax imposed on legal documents (in this case, documents related to the transfer of property) currently the stamp duty is JMD$5,000.00, while the transfer tax is charged on the value of the property being transferred.

Here's how the Stamp Office factors into the conveyance process:

Assessment of Stamp Duty and Transfer Tax: Once the sales agreement is executed, the documents related to the property transfer must be submitted to the Stamp Office for the assessment of stamp duty and transfer tax. The value of these taxes is determined based on the transaction value or the property's market value, whichever is higher.

Payment of Duties: Before the transfer of property can be legally recognized, the assessed stamp duty and transfer tax must be paid. The Stamp Office provides a stamp certificate or a receipt indicating that the taxes have been duly paid. This step is crucial as unstamped or improperly stamped documents are not legally effective for property transfer purposes.

Stamping and Endorsement: After the payment of duties, the Stamp Office stamps the documents, signifying that they are legally valid and that all necessary taxes have been paid. This process includes the endorsement of the transfer documents, which is essential for the subsequent registration of the property in the buyer's name.

Calculation of Taxes and Duties: The transfer tax is typically a percentage of the property's appraised value or the value of its holding. It stands at 2% sale price or market value whichever is higher, while stamp duty is calculated based on the value of the transaction or the property value. Currently, the rate of stamp duty as of the writing of this book is a fixed charge mentioned as JMD $5000.These tax rate can vary and may be subject to changes based on government policy.

Adjustments and Exemptions: In certain circumstances, adjustments to the assessed duties and taxes may be necessary, such as when specific exemptions or reductions apply. For instance, beneficiaries under specific government programs may qualify for reduced rates or exemptions.

All the government entities are indispensable steps in the conveyance process, ensuring the legal validity of the property transfer and compliance with Jamaican tax laws. It's advisable for buyers and sellers to engage legal and financial professionals to navigate this process efficiently, ensuring all requirements are met and facilitating a smooth transfer of ownership.

CHAPTER 3

Owning vs. Renting

As we step into the realm of homeownership, we encounter a myriad of stories, each unique in its journey. From unexpected turns of fate to moments of divine intervention, the quest for a home to call our own unfolds in diverse ways. Whether sparked by eviction, guided by mentors, or propelled by faith, the path to owning a home is a testament to resilience, determination, and the human spirit. I now share my journey.

After a brief period in the army, life, with its ironic twists, led me and my daughter back to the same house where I had found refuge on the night I was cast out by my father. We rented a single room, sharing amenities like the bathroom, kitchen, living area, and laundry. Initially, my rent was JMD $500, but it soon doubled to JMD $1,000 when the landlord decided to increase it significantly. Faced with this dilemma, I consulted a friend about finding another rental. Her advice shifted my perspective dramatically—she suggested I buy a house instead. Around the same time, I was reading "The Richest Man in Babylon" by George S. Clason, which reinforced this advice with its own wisdom on homeownership. The book stresses the importance of owning your own home, beautifully summarized in the quote: "No man's family can fully enjoy life unless they have a plot of ground where their children can play in their own backyard." This essentially means that true happiness for a family comes from having their own home, complete with a yard for the children to play in.

Motivated by my friend's encouragement, my need for my daughter to avoid the hardships I faced, and the advice from the book "The

Richest Man in Babylon," I set out on a mission to buy a house. My journey to homeownership was anything but direct. I explored many neighborhoods, and in my naivety, I often prioritized the area over what I could realistically afford, leading to an exhausting and sometimes disheartening search. The true challenge, however, wasn't a lack of suitable homes but rather that my efforts were misguided, focusing too much on location rather than affordability. In other words, i was looking for apples in the orange field.

Guidance can come from the most unexpected places. For me, it was a coworker and my boss who pointed me towards a promising opportunity at Fairview Park, a new development in Spanish Town. I visited their Island Homes ltd office on Hope Road during one lunch break and discovered that 2-bedroom, 1-bathroom houses were being sold for a reasonable $175,000. Thanks to the financial lessons from "The Richest Man in Babylon," which advises saving 10% of your income and making profitable investments, I had already saved up the required 15% deposit. After placing my deposit, I received a Sale Agreement that was as perplexing as a foreign language to me, reflecting how little I understood of its contents at the time.

It was the same friend who demystified the Sale Agreement for me, emphasizing the need for a mortgage. Yet, every door I knocked on—banks, the National Housing Trust—seemed to close in my face, telling me I didn't qualify. Undeterred, I traversed far and wide, my resolve fortified by constant prayer, seeking the solution that felt just beyond reach. Then, as if by a stroke of divine intervention, while seeking insurance for my mother who suffered her first stroke while living in the USA. It was at that moment the universe opened up to help me. I was led to a gentleman who stepped forward to co-sign my loan. Ever since I became a firm believer in divine intervention and a greater force in the universe guiding us.

This chapter, rich with lessons and pivotal moments, mirrors the experiences that future homeowners or renters may encounter at their own crossroads of decision. When that time comes for you to decide between buying and renting, consider these essential factors:

When deciding whether to buy or rent a home, it's crucial to thoroughly assess your financial situation and understand what you can realistically afford. This includes considering upfront costs like the down payment and closing fees, as well as ongoing expenses such as mortgage payments, property taxes, maintenance, and insurance.

Reflect on your long-term plans as well. Homeownership is generally more beneficial if you plan to stay in one location for a considerable amount of time, given its nature as a long-term investment. Additionally, take the time to research the housing market in your desired areas to determine whether current market conditions favor buying or renting.

Your lifestyle and personal preferences also play a critical role in this decision. Owning a home provides stability for you and your family and gives you the freedom to make modifications to your living space. On the other hand, renting offers less responsibility for maintenance and more flexibility to move, which can be advantageous if you anticipate changes in your living situation or job location in the near future.

Finally, consider your readiness to handle home maintenance. Owning a home means you'll be responsible for upkeep, whereas renting generally means most maintenance issues will be managed by your landlord. The choice between buying and renting involves weighing these personal, financial, and lifestyle factors carefully to decide which option best suits your needs and circumstances.

Let's now delve into some more advantages of buying a home:

Homeownership stands out as a beacon of family stability and security. It provides you with the liberty to tailor your environment without seeking approval from a landlord. This freedom allows for personalization and renovations that can reflect your style and meet your family's needs. More importantly, it offers a stable environment where children can flourish, providing them with a sense of belonging and a secure backdrop for their growth.

Financially, buying a home is a significant investment that facilitates the building of equity. As you pay down your mortgage, you increase the portion of the property that you truly own. Additionally, over time, your home may appreciate in value, potentially yielding a substantial return on investment should you choose to sell. This aspect of homeownership not only secures your financial future but can also contribute to your wealth.

Moreover, there are potential tax advantages to owning a home. Homeowners may benefit from deductions on mortgage interest and property taxes, which can provide considerable savings when it's time to file tax returns. These financial benefits underscore the practical perks of owning rather than renting a home, further enhancing the appeal of homeownership as a wise long-term choice.

Additionally, homeowners should be aware of market dynamics. While property values can fluctuate, they often trend upward over time, potentially enhancing your investment. Even though there's a risk of a market downturn leading to owing more than your home's current value, historically, real estate markets tend to recover and grow, presenting long-term benefits and equity gains.

Renting a Home: Advantages and Considerations

Renting a home offers increased flexibility, making it ideal for those in transitional life stages or with careers that require frequent mobility. It allows you to move without the long-term commitment associated with a mortgage.

The initial costs of renting are typically lower than buying, and limited to just a security deposit and the first month's rent. Additionally, renters benefit from not having to handle property maintenance and repairs, as these responsibilities usually fall to the landlord, alleviating both physical and financial burdens.

However, there are also important considerations to keep in mind: Renting does not allow you to build equity; your monthly payments benefit the landlord, not your financial assets. There's also the risk of rent increases and the potential need to move unexpectedly if the landlord decides not to renew the agreement, opts to sell the property, or, as what happened to me, significantly raises the rent.. Additionally, renting can limit your ability to personalize your living space. Landlords often impose restrictions on making modifications to the property, which can affect how much you can make a rental feel like home.

Deciding Whether to Rent or Buy

Deciding whether to rent or buy a home is a significant decision that hinges on various personal and financial factors. Are you financially prepared for homeownership? It's crucial to evaluate if you have the necessary savings for a down payment and closing costs, and whether you can sustain the ongoing financial responsibilities that come with owning a home, such as mortgage payments, property taxes, insurance, and maintenance costs. Moreover, ensure that your income is stable and robust enough to support these commitments over the long term.

Consider your credit record as well. Is it robust enough to secure favorable mortgage rates, or would it be more prudent to rent while you work on improving your financial standing? Additionally, think about how homeownership fits into your broader financial strategies. Do you view buying a home primarily as an investment, or do you value the liquidity and financial flexibility that renting provides, allowing you to allocate funds to other ventures?

Your lifestyle preferences also play a crucial role in this decision. If you anticipate staying in the same location for many years, buying might make more financial sense. However, if your career or personal life requires mobility, renting could be more advantageous due to the high upfront costs associated with purchasing a home. Reflect on how long you plan to stay in the area and whether you prefer the stability of owning your home or the flexibility to move without the obligations of property sale.

It's also important to consider the current real estate market conditions and how they align with your personal and financial goals. Is the market favorable for buyers, or are high prices and competitive environments leaning you towards renting? Think about your living space needs—does your situation warrant buying a home, or would a rental suffice? Assess your plans for family, work-from-home needs, and social life, which all influence the amount of space you require.

Ultimately, it's crucial to recognize that your home-buying decisions will hinge on what you can realistically afford. It's not practical to consider properties in areas that exceed your budget. I learned this lesson myself after a year of searching in locations that were beyond my financial reach, until my coworkers directed me to more reasonably priced homes in Fairview Park.

Therefore, evaluating whether to buy or rent a home involves a careful analysis of both personal and financial factors. All the considerations mentioned previously can be scrutinized in a structured manner. However, irrespective of the above considerations at the core of my belief, deeply felt and sincerely held, is the conviction that like George Clayson says in his book "The richest man in Babylon" **Make of thy dwelling a profitable investment "Own thy own home."**

and for me that means as soon as you start earning. To me, homeownership represents the most meaningful investment one can make, a commitment worthy of a significant portion of one's income.

Also, over time, I've come to understand that real estate is a legacy, enduring beyond a lifetime, where nearly everything else we buy eventually deteriorates or becomes obsolete. The sense of fulfillment and warmth that comes from owning the space where you live is unparalleled. It's a feeling of profound joy and comfort that greets me and my children each time we open our door.

My own transition from grappling with rent hikes as a tenant to becoming a homeowner has been a journey rich with learning. It taught me not only about the intricacies of the housing market but also underscored the value of persistence, the ability to adapt, and the critical nature of making choices that are in harmony with one's own life and financial plans. This mirrors the wisdom found in "The Richest Man in Babylon," emphasizing that the choice between buying and renting is not just a financial decision but a deeply personal one. It demands a thoughtful assessment of numerous essential factors, guiding us to a decision that aligns with our long-term aspirations and well-being.

CHAPTER 4

Getting Started: Preparing for Your Home Purchase

When you have reached the decision to buy a house to make your home, you'll quickly realize it's a big financial step, way bigger than your usual shopping for clothes or food. Often, it can use up all the money you have, and maybe even more, which is why being prepared is so important.

Some people think I just got lucky to buy my first house when I was 23.In my favorite book, "The Richest Man in Babylon",as discussed in the chapter "the goddess of good luck" refers to the concept of luck as a force that favors those who are prepared and who work hard. This idea is encapsulated in the book's teachings that good fortune and success are not merely matters of chance, but rather the results of specific actions and attitudes that align with the laws of prosperity that Clason outlines through his Babylonian parables.

Having embraced the financial wisdom from "The Richest Man in Babylon," I had already ingrained the habit of saving 10% of my income and maintaining a firm grip on my expenses. My savings were in place, and I had a clear understanding of my financial health and position. While I was positioned well in terms of saving and budgeting, I recognize that not everyone might be at this stage. So, in the following sections, I'll share strategies to help you prepare your finances for the home-buying process.

For those just starting out, or if you find yourself unprepared when the chance to purchase a home arises, I will also delve into various methods you might explore to gather the necessary funds. Whether you're building your savings from scratch or seeking avenues to accelerate your financial readiness, these insights aim to equip you with the tools needed to move toward homeownership confidently.

Assessing Your Financial Readiness

Before taking the plunge into homeownership, it's crucial to evaluate your financial health and readiness. This assessment is the foundation for a successful home purchase, ensuring that you can not only buy a house but also afford to keep it over the long term. Here's what to consider when planning to buy a home.

To begin, it's essential to compare your savings against the amount required for a down payment. A larger down payment typically results in lower monthly mortgage payments. Additionally, be prepared for costs beyond the purchase price, including closing costs, moving expenses, and maintenance and repair costs.

A detailed financial plan for homeownership should encompass not only the initial costs of buying a home but also ongoing expenses such as property taxes, homeowners insurance, and maintenance. These factors are vital for a full understanding of the financial responsibilities of home ownership.

For financing, it's advisable to speak with loan officers who can assess your current income and expenses to determine your borrowing capacity. Lenders will look at your debt-to-income ratio to evaluate your ability to manage monthly payments. Lowering your existing debt can improve your chances of getting a loan and secure more favorable terms.

Understanding Your Credit History

Your credit history is a critical factor in the home buying process, as it influences your ability to secure a mortgage and the terms of that mortgage, including the interest rates. Your credit score is a numerical expression based on an analysis of your credit files, representing your creditworthiness. Lenders use this score to determine the risk of lending you money. A higher credit score often translates to lower interest rates on your mortgage, which can save you significant amounts of money over the life of the loan. If your credit score is less than ideal, it's advisable to spend some time improving it before applying for a mortgage. This can involve paying down existing debts, making all your current payments on time, and avoiding new credit inquiries or high credit card balances.

Debt-to-Income Ratio (DTI):

Another crucial factor lenders consider is your debt-to-income ratio, which is the percentage of your gross monthly income that goes towards paying debts. A lower DTI shows lenders that you have a good balance between debt and income, making you less of a financial risk and more likely to secure favorable mortgage terms. To calculate your DTI, divide your total monthly debt payments by your gross monthly income. Most lenders prefer a DTI of 45% or less, with no more than 40% of that debt going towards servicing a mortgage or rent.

Income Verification

Lenders will verify your income to ensure you have the financial means to meet your mortgage obligations. This process typically involves reviewing your wage statements, tax returns, and other documents that prove your income. Consistency in your income can be as important as the amount when assessing your financial stability.

Improving Your Credit History

If your credit history isn't in the best shape, taking steps to improve it can be crucial before purchasing a home. This can include consolidating debts to lower interest rates, avoiding new debt, and keeping older credit accounts open to lengthen your credit history. Also, regularly checking your credit report for errors and disputing any inaccuracies can help improve your score.

Credit Utilization

Maintaining a low credit utilization ratio can also help boost your credit score. This ratio measures how much of your available credit you are using; the lower the utilization, the better it is for your score.

Evaluating your financial readiness is the cornerstone of making a home purchase. It's about transforming the dream of homeownership into a tangible plan with actionable steps. The first significant milestone in this quest is often accumulating a necessary down payment, which is typically 5 to 10 percent of the home's purchase price. Sometimes the opportunity to purchase a home comes before you are ready, when you have no or very little funds to make use of the opportunity. To assist with this, I've identified several strategies you might consider to increase your down payment fund:

National Housing Trust (NHT)

The NHT will allow you to use contributions not yet due for refund to offset your deposit under the Contribution Refund Towards Deposit (CRTD) facility.

In recognizing this challenge faced by many prospective home buyers, the National Housing Trust (NHT), in 2010, introduced the Contribution Refund Towards Deposit (CRTD) loan. All qualified contributors purchasing a house, a lot, or building a residential property that will be funded by an NHT loan, may borrow up to 100% of their available contributions not yet due for refund.

The NHT will allow you to use contributions not yet due for refund to offset your deposit up to six years contribution can be used for the following:-

1. To assist with the deposit (refers to the initial down payment) of the said property.

2. To assist with closing costs and/or shortfall on purchase price, legal fees (including purchaser's attorney's fees).

3. To assist with payments for surveyor's identification reports and/or structural engineer's

4. To assist with start-up funding for construction projects as follows:

1. Site Confirmation Report

2. Bill of Quantities (BOQ)

3. Cost of Excavation

4. Clearing of land

5. Lining out of building

6. Pegging of boundaries

7. Any other construction-related costs approved by the Leadership Team

This facility is not regular contribution refund. Please feel free to reach out to me or NHT for advice on how to access this facility to use as part or all of your deposit requirements.

Credit Union and National Housing Trust

The National Housing Trust, NHT, has made improvements to the Housing Microfinance Loan Programme which allows contributors to access financing from approved credit unions towards a wider range of housing expenses.

Funds accessed under the Programme can be used for among other things: deposit, construction preliminaries, for example, valuation report, surveyor's ID report and land purchase. The approved list of credit unions is: C&W Co-operative Credit Union, EduCom, Jamaica Police Co-operative Credit Union, Public Sector Employees Co-operative Credit Union, Lasco/Isle Employees Partners Co-operative Credit Union, Essential Emergency Services Co-operative Credit Union, Jamaica Defence Force Co-operative Credit Union, First Heritage Co-operative Credit Union, Trelawny Co-operative Credit Union, Manchester Co-operative Credit Union, Gateway Co-operative Credit Union, and PWU Co-operative Credit Union.

The Jamaica Police Co-operative Credit Union

[https://jpccu.com.jm/home-store/loans-2/easy-home/]

If you are a member of the Jamaica Constabulary Force you can access a loan facility to pay deposit payment under the following loan facility:

The Easy Home Loan is a joint venture between the National Housing Trust and Jamaica Police Co-operative Credit Union Ltd. designed for police members who are NHT contributors to access funds for as low as 6% per annum.

The purposes can be any housing related expenses. Examples include (but are not limited to):

- Down payment on property

- Legal fees for purchase of property

DOCUMENTS REQUIRED

- Valid ID & TRN

- Proof of Address

- Last Two Months Payslips

- Proof of Ownership of Property

- Application Form

The maximum that can be applied for at any one time is $850,000.00 however the limit any member can have on this facility is $1,500,000.00. Members can also apply for an unsecured loan.

The Jamaica Defence Force Credit Union

If you are a member of the Jamaica Defence Force you can access a loan facility for deposit payment under the following loan facility:

[https://jdfcreditunion.com/loans/]

The JDF CU introduced the KASH Loan, you can get up to $750,000.00 unsecured with a repayment period of 60 months or revolving at attractive interest rates.

Insurance Policies

If you hold insurance policies, you may inquire about the potential cash value or dividends that can be redeemed, utilizing the funds as a contribution to your deposit.

Personal Savings

Build a disciplined saving plan by setting aside a portion of income into a dedicated savings account. Automate transfers to make saving more consistent.

Family and Friends

Reach out to family members for contributions or loans to support the deposit. Highlight the collective impact, as the saying goes, "Every mickle makes a muckle," and keep in mind the wisdom of one one cocol full basket."

Employer Assistance

Check with employers for any home-buying assistance programs, benefits, or low-interest loans for employees. Some companies offer financial perks to support home purchases.

Personal Loans

Explore the option of securing a personal loan to cover a portion of the deposit. Verify deposit loan offerings from financial institutions such as Scotia and Jamaica National. Click the links below to be connected to a loan officer.

Side Hustles, Part-Time Work or Overtime Work

Take on a part-time job, work overtime or explore side hustles to supplement income specifically earmarked for the home deposit.

Crowdfunding

Utilize crowdfunding platforms to seek contributions from friends, family, or online communities that support the goal of homeownership.

Redundancy payments, Bonus and Back pay packages

Allocate unexpected financial windfalls, such as tax refunds, work bonuses, or redundancy packages, to make up the deposit fund.

Credit Card

If you possess a credit card with available credit, you have the option to obtain cash by using the card's PIN and withdrawing funds from an ATM. Be aware that this will be at a high interest rate.

Each option has its pros and cons, so it's important to consider what's best for your financial situation and long-term goals. Always feel free to seek advice from financial advisors or the institutions themselves to make the most informed decision.

You might be feeling a bit overwhelmed right now, wondering if owning a home is really in the cards for you. Don't worry—keep reading I'll show you it's definitely possible!

CHAPTER 5

Searching for the Right Home

Aunt Dolly's Wisdom - Understanding Money and Value**

Being Ready Before You Leap

When I first thought about buying a house because my friend said it was better than renting, I had no idea what I was doing. While i was ready financially with the deposit, My income wasn't ready to secure a mortgage. I liked lots of houses, but the lenders kept saying no. It was a tough time, and it stressed me out a lot. Aunt Dolly always said to shop in places where your money can actually buy something. For houses, this means knowing your budget and sticking to it, so you don't end up feeling defeated.

Like that day I went shoe shopping on Constant Spring Road, drawn by shiny, expensive shoes that I couldn't afford. I felt pretty down about it. But then, I found another shop where the shoes were just as nice but more in my budget. What Aunt Dolly used to say, "Things only seem too expensive when you can't afford them." This is very important for buying a house. You must know how much you can spend before falling in love with a place that you can't afford oops or "that's way too expensive."

Reflecting on the price of shoes opens a gateway to a much deeper story, one that begins with Aunt Dolly. Cast out at 15, I found myself adrift from place to place until I landed on her welcoming doorstep. Despite her modest means, she shared her space, her heart, and, most importantly, her insights with me. We always went supermarket shopping with her pension in hand. I'd often grumble about the cost of everything. With a twinkle in her eye, Aunt Dolly would retort, "Claudia, everything seems expensive when you have no money in your pocket!"

Our banter was more than mere conversation; it was Aunt Dolly imparting life-altering wisdom. She insisted that my view of what was expensive would transform once I had money of my own. More than that, she taught me a lesson in self-worth and decision-making: to navigate life and its supermarkets with the money I have, ensuring I never felt downcast or diminished by trying to buy what I couldn't afford.

Aunt Dolly's philosophy was simple yet profound. "Shop where your money will take you," she advised, instilling in me the power of living within my means while still striving for a richer life and not just material wealth. Her wisdom was a guiding star, teaching me that true value isn't in the price tag but in the joy and security we find and that real happiness comes from living within our means and finding joy in what we can afford.

Buying a home is not just a financial transaction; it's an emotional voyage, filled with dreams, aspirations, and occasionally heartbreaks. My own journey peppered with lessons from Aunt Dolly underscores the importance of patience, perspective, and preparedness in navigating this path. Understanding Money and Value, here is what I learned.

The Lesson of Perspective

Much like my mixed experiences in shoe shopping, the journey to homeownership often swings between excitement and despair. Aunt Dolly taught me that "everything will look expensive because you have no money in your pocket." This wisdom is crucial when house hunting. Understanding and accepting your financial reality can prevent the heartache of falling in love with homes out of your reach. Begin your search with a clear-eyed assessment of your budget, getting pre-approved for a mortgage and adding up your savings and other cash investments. Also, it's important to know how much the deposit and closing costs for the house purchase and the fees the bank, the building society, or credit union will charge to give you the loan. Count these costs to understand what you truly can afford.

The Lesson of Preparedness

Disappointment marked my initial foray into the housing market, driven by a friend's encouragement to buy or rent,. I liked many homes, but the bank repeatedly told me I didn't qualify for them. This period was mentally taxing, leading to profound stress and even physical manifestations of it. Aunt Dolly's principle of shopping "where your money will take you" is vital here. Before starting your search, thoroughly understand your financial standing and the mortgage process. This preparation can significantly reduce the stress and emotional toll of house hunting.

The Lesson of Resilience

Staying strong trying to buy a house got even harder when my mom got sick. The journey took a toll on me, mentally and physically. It was a really low point. But it's in the hard times that you must persevere, and it was during this challenging period that I accidentally discovered an unexpected opportunity that ultimately allowed me to become a homeowner. Aunt Dolly believed in never giving up, even when things look grim. For anyone trying to buy their first home, remember it is about hanging in there, even when it gets rough.

Aunt Dolly's wisdom—to adapt, to pivot, to keep moving forward, and to make the best with what you have—was instrumental. I also played netball to the Business House level. My role in the game was Wing Attack (WA) and I energetically executed in that position. That game teaches us to pivot, seek openings on your blind side, pass the ball with accuracy, and keep moving forward toward the goal. The process of buying a home is quite similar in numerous ways, Its about resilience, keeping faith, finding people to help you, and keep pivoting till you find the opportunity, even in the least expected places.

The Lesson of Finding Value

To Aunt Dolly, finding value went beyond the price tag—it was about the joy and satisfaction that something adds to your life. This principle is especially relevant when purchasing a home. It's important to consider not just the cost but also the peace, stability, belonging, and potential that a home could bring. Often, the best value comes from homes that might not check every single box but provide a solid base for a happy and fulfilling life.

My Aunt Dolly's practical wisdom has been a guiding light through the complexities of my life, including the intricate process of buying a home. Her teachings extended beyond theoretical advice, encompassing essential aspects like budgeting, preparing thoroughly before house hunting, and maintaining resilience in the face of challenges. Embarking on this journey may seem daunting, but it's ultimately a rewarding quest for a place to call your own, informed by the wisdom of those who have traversed similar paths before.

For many, the excitement of viewing potential homes is a thrilling start to the home-buying process. However, this is not actually the first step. Before you even consider scheduling viewings, there's crucial groundwork to be laid.

Assuming you've secured your down payment and mortgage preapproval among other financial preparations, the real first step is to strategically map out your budget and identify where homes within your price range are located. This involves a practical assessment of how much you can afford to spend and determining the "House Market" where you'll begin your search.

Consider the parameters of your search area— Are you interested in a detached house, an apartment, a townhouse, or perhaps a plot of land for building? Will your new home be in the bustling heart of a parish capital, or are you drawn to the tranquility of the countryside? These are all critical questions to answer as you define the scope and focus of your home search.

Choosing Your Path to Homeownership: Building Lots, Developments, or Existing Homes

Homeownership comes with big choices, like:

1. Buying land and building your own home.

2. Investing in a new housing development.

3. Buying an already built home.

Each option has different pros and cons that will affect where you live, your money, and how you live for many years.

Building on Your Own Land

Customization is the hallmark of building your own home. This route allows you to tailor every detail from the floor plan to the finishes, buy every nail and screw ensuring your home perfectly reflects your personal style and meets your needs. The freedom to control costs can also be advantageous as well as selecting materials and design elements within your budget can keep expenses manageable. Also, the initial deposit is lower since the cost of the land is lower than the cost of the house. However, the building process is time-intensive and can be fraught with unforeseen expenses, such as construction delays or rise in the cost of material due to inflation and the constant challenge of finding good tradesmen, which can test your patience and budget.

Investing in New Housing Developments

New housing developments provide homes with modern amenities and technologies, ensuring an energy-efficient and contemporary living environment. These developments often feature communal facilities like swimming pools and gyms, enhancing your lifestyle within the community. Additionally, buying a home in these areas typically includes a six-month grace period from the developer, which gives you reassurance about the home's quality and upkeep.

However, there are some downsides to consider. These communities may lack the unique character of a custom-built home, come with high maintenance fees, and impose numerous restrictions. Often located on the outskirts of parish capital, living in these developments can sometimes affect your daily commute and access to essential services like hospitals, universities, and commercial centers.

Purchasing Existing Homes - For Sale By Owner

Buying an existing home can be the most straightforward path to homeownership, offering the immediate charm of established neighborhoods and the potential for rapid occupancy. These homes are often in mature communities with established infrastructure and a strong sense of belonging. For those willing to invest in renovations, there's significant potential to increase the home's value. However, older properties might require more maintenance, limited life expectancy and could be less energy-efficient, posing additional costs over time. The competitive housing market also means you might face bidding wars, driving up prices and testing your resolve.

My Journey

Buying a New House

Embarking on the journey of buying a home brings a unique set of experiences and challenges, whether it's purchasing from a developer, building on your own land, or buying an existing property. My initial venture into homeownership was through a developer called Island Homes who built the Fairview Park Community in Spanish Town. The allure of a brand-new home and neighborhood was instantly appealing. However, the newness came with its own challenges. The home required additions such as security grills, curtain rods, fencing, driveways, landscaping, a water tank, and ceiling fans—each requiring time, attention, and further investment.

Adding to all that the unpredictability of life, an unforgettable episode from the early 1990s comes to mind. One particular day, marked by severe weather, remains etched in my memory. As I left New Kingston with my young daughter, we found ourselves caught in a sudden, relentless downpour that turned the streets into rivers. Public transportation had ceased, leaving us soaked, stranded, and at the mercy of the elements.

At this juncture, our story takes an unexpected turn. A man, driving a pickup truck, noticed our plight and offered us a ride to Spanish Town. This was no ordinary commute, but a voyage through a storm, navigating through flooded streets that challenged the very boundaries between land and water. But we soldiered on, with unyielding determination, the universe steering us through the downpour, attempting various routes in a bid to find passable roads. Our destination, Fairview Park, had transformed into an expansive, makeshift river. The journey required charity, and when the Pickup Truck could no longer serve as our chariot, we transitioned to foot. The man, embodying the spirit of heroism, carried my daughter through the water, ensuring our safe arrival at our doorstep.

The aftermath of the storm left my home besieged by water, leading us to a night spent using towels and newspaper as makeshift efforts against the flood. This ordeal sparked a resolute determination in me to save my money and fortify my home against future storms, culminating in the construction of a significant six feet back wall.

Fast forward to an encounter on March 15, 2024, (right about the time I'm writing this book). The bustling environment of New Kingston, a twist of fate allowed me to cross paths with the kind stranger once again. Our chance meeting beside CIBC Bank reignited memories of that chaotic day, and we shared a moment of laughter, gratitude, reflection and of course, we exchanged numbers.

This experience serves as a testament to the unexpected acts of kindness that can emerge from adverse situations, highlighting the resilience of the human spirit in the face of challenges. It's a reminder that underlines the importance of community, preparedness, and the indomitable will to overcome and adapt. This story is not merely about surviving a storm but about the profound connections and personal growth that can arise from the most trying of circumstances.

Buying Land and Building my own Home

Then came the unique adventure of building my own home, leading me down an entirely different path. During one visit to the construction site of my house, the weather suddenly turned hostile. A fierce downpour seemed to target me personally. I sought shelter in the unfinished building I was constructing, but even the concrete roof above betrayed me, allowing water to seep through every conceivable crack. Ironically, I was there to discuss additional funding requests from the contractor to complete the project. As I stood trapped by the relentless rain, with no place to go and unable to move, I turned inward, silently praying for resilience and wisdom to weather this literal and figurative storm..

As the downpour continued unabated, I faced a critical decision. With each moment, as the situation worsened, it became clear that a change in strategy was imperative. Driven by the urgent challenges presented by the weather itself, I decided to take a more hands-on approach in managing the project. With a mixture of determination and trepidation, I made the tough decision to let go of my contractor and assume the daunting role of managing the construction myself. This marked a pivotal shift in my journey, taking direct control to navigate the challenges ahead. This moment was not just about taking control of a faltering project; it was a testament to the necessity of adaptability and leadership in the face of unforeseen challenges. It marked a significant pivot point, both for the project at hand and for my personal growth as a determined individual ready to confront and navigate the storm that life, quite literally, can throw. This experience tested my resilience, as I navigated the complexities of managing tradesmen and ensuring my vision came to life. This chapter of my life was so impactful that it inspired me to deepen my knowledge in the field. I enrolled in HEART TRUST NTA to study Building

Construction at levels 1 and 2, an education that has been invaluable in subsequent building projects.

Buying a For Sale By owner Property : The Fixer-Upper Triumph

One leisurely Sunday afternoon, as I perused the Sunday Gleaner, my eyes landed on an ad that sent my heart racing—a 3-bedroom apartment for sale in New Kingston. In a burst of excitement, I rallied my daughter, who by this time was a student at the University of Technology (UTech) and we hailed a taxi to the address.

Arriving at the complex, we were greeted by a building that had seen better days, and the apartment itself bore the signs of neglect. Silicone and caulking spider-webbed across the bathroom surfaces, the windows fought against closure, and the kitchen,while outdated, held a certain charm of functionality. It featured two window AC units—a small comfort against Kingston's heat.

While my daughter engaged with the seller,nephew a fellow UTech attendee, exchanging college tales, I took the opportunity to roam the space. Despite its rundown state, I saw potential where others might see despair. The asking price sat at a modest JMD $2.8 million, suspiciously low, stirring my instincts. Just four weeks prior—a similar apartment in the same complex was listed at JMD $4 million—a sharp difference that explained my urgency. With the vision of a diamond in the rough firmly in my mind, The thrill of real estate adventure coursed through my veins as I negotiated a stellar deal, securing not just a promising apartment but also a three-piece chair set, an electric stove, and a dining room table and 4 chairs.

As we prepared to leave, I confidently told the young man to consider the apartment as good as sold—I would return with the deposit in the morning. Truth be told, it was a bluff; my pockets were as empty as the apartment's charm was hidden. I left the complex with a plan brewing. Though my wallet didn't match my ambition, I've always believed where there's a will, there's a way. And so, with a night ahead to conjure up a solution, the stage was set for yet another exhilarating leap into the world of real estate.

The following morning, I was at the bank's doors by 8 AM, ready to march straight to victory, or more accurately, a loan officer's desk. With determination etched across my face and perhaps a touch of dramatic flair, I declared my mission to the loan officer: "I need JMD 300k for a deposit on an apartment and I'm not leaving without it." Maybe it was my conviction or the fierce force of my will that set the officer into swift action, but in moments, a Scotia Plan loan was materializing before my eyes. The seller's lawyer was soon on the line, setting wheels into motion and later with a mortgage from Jamaica National Building Society the stage was set for me to become the proud owner of my very first apartment.

But, as life loves to remind us, the journey was far from over. My daughter and I armed ourselves with cleaners and scrubbers, ready to make the apartment sparkle for its future tenant. Yet, as soon as we started cleaning the bathroom and turned on the shower to wash the bath, a loud banging erupted at the front door. As I opened the door, "It's raining in my apartment!" exclaimed the man from downstairs. Following him to his apartment, I witnessed a downpour in his bathroom—water cascaded from the ceiling. My heart sank; my dreams of quick rental income now seemed as drenched as the man's bathroom floor. Back upstairs, my eyes darted across every inch of the bathroom in the apartment, but the culprit behind the leak was elusive. The only way forward was clear, albeit daunting: a full demolition of the bathroom.

With determination in my heart, I sought additional financing from Jamaica National. As the bathroom was dismantled, we uncovered a shattered ground trap beneath the bath drain—a testament to the previous owner's failed repair attempts. I could almost feel her exasperation as plumber after plumber failed to fix the issue, ultimately pushing her towards selling the property to escape the headache. Yet, I was undeterred and plunged into the renovations with vigor. The bathroom was completely overhauled with new fixtures, fittings, and fresh tiles. The kitchen received a modern makeover, and I also installed new windows and a new air conditioning unit in the bedroom and new paint was the final touch. The apartment was not just repaired; it was transformed into a beacon of resilience and potential. Shortly after listing it on the market, it was rented out, proving that persistence and hard work truly pay off.

As for purchasing an existing home I soon realised I had purchased a 'raining' apartment, that brought its own set of challenges, predominantly in the form of repairs, renovations, additional funds and delay in renting the property. Reflecting on these experiences, it becomes evident that rain and water have been more than just natural phenomena in my life they've acted as catalysts for learning profound lessons. These elements have shown me that homeownership transcends the mere exchange of finances for property. It embodies a deep-seated commitment to a project that demands relentless dedication, an openness to learning, and, occasionally and sometimes, a significant personal transformation.

From these experiences, the overarching lesson is clear: embarking on the journey of buying a home, in whatever form it takes, is as much about building a life as it is about constructing a physical structure. It's about readiness to tackle unexpected challenges, the willingness to learn and adapt, and above all, the courage to take on the responsibilities that come with turning a house into a home.

In addition, whether facing the blank slate of a newly developed property to the complexities of building from the ground up, or the surprises of an existing home, each path offers unique rewards that extend far beyond the walls that house us. Once you've decided upon your criteria, call your real estate agent. Let them know what you're looking for and what your price range is. They will get to work on your behalf, shortlisting the properties that might suit your criteria so you can start your viewing from there. Then comes the fun part: Finding that perfect home you've been dreaming of.

CHAPTER 6

Viewing Properties

Your journey toward homeownership should align with your personal preferences, financial situation, and aspirations. Whereas, building a home offers unparalleled customization but demands patience and a flexible budget. New developments cater to those seeking modern amenities and a community lifestyle, albeit with some sacrifices in location and uniqueness. Meanwhile, existing homes appeal to those looking for character, convenience, and the opportunity to infuse a property with their personal touch, despite potential maintenance and efficiency concerns. Here are a few things to incorporate in this stage of the journey .

Allocate Sufficient Time

When viewing homes, it's crucial to allow enough time to thoroughly examine the property. This is potentially your future home, so a brief five-minute walk-through won't suffice. Plan for at least an hour to explore the space, checking every closet and corner, to truly understand if it meets your needs.

Be Detailed in Your Inspection

Along with setting aside enough time for a viewing, it's important to be meticulous during the inspection. Open every drawer, cabinet, and cupboard. Check for signs of termite damage or leaky roofs. Since buying a home is a major financial commitment, you need to know exactly what you are considering purchasing. Sometimes, furniture or decor is strategically placed to cover up issues, so do not hesitate to look behind and beneath to fully assess the condition. If you are not impressed initially, a brief overview might be all you need. However, if the home shows promise, take the opportunity to investigate every nook and cranny.

Verify What's Included

Make sure to confirm what items come with the property. Determine whether features like ceiling fans, fixtures, camera systems, water tanks, or solar water heaters are included in the sale. If you decide to make an offer, specify in writing which items you expect to be part of the deal to avoid any misunderstandings later.

Keep Emotions at Bay

When you first view a home, it's important not to become too attached immediately. Try to view the property objectively as a structure to inspect thoroughly, rather than something you're already emotionally invested in. Rapid emotional attachment can cloud your judgment, making you overlook potential issues that you might notice if you weren't emotionally involved. If you become attached too quickly, it can compromise your ability to negotiate calmly and objectively.

View More Than Once

If a property catches your interest, make sure to visit it multiple times. Returning at different times of the day will help you catch any potential issues and get a real feel for the neighborhood. For example, a street that seems quiet in the late morning might be a busy thoroughfare in the early morning and late afternoon. Multiple visits can help you understand traffic patterns and noise levels throughout the day.

Let Your Agent Do the Job

Always visit properties with your real estate agent for safety and expertise. If you find a property on your own that your agent hasn't mentioned, it might not meet all your criteria. If you still want to view it, provide your agent with the address and phone number. let them arrange the viewing. This ensures that all aspects of the property viewing are handled professionally and safely.Your agent can then arrange a proper viewing for you, together, without the owner being present.

Assessing the Condition of the Property

When considering a home for purchase, it's crucial to closely examine the condition of the property.

Structural Integrity: Begin by assessing whether the home is structurally sound. Walk through the interior and inspect walls and ceilings for any cracks. While minor hairline cracks can be normal, look for signs of more serious structural issues like significant cracking or bowing walls. If such problems are evident, it's wise to bring in a structural engineer for a detailed assessment. Also, check for any signs of a leaking roof, and inquire about the duration and plans for repair of such issues.

Mold Inspection: observe the presence of mold, which can be both costly and challenging to eradicate. Don't rely solely on visual signs; use your sense of smell to detect any musty odors, which often accompany mold even when it is not immediately visible. Inspect ceilings, basement areas, and the base of walls for flaking plaster, watermarks, or fresh paint that may indicate past water issues. Ensure to thoroughly inspect the ceiling and skirting boards for any signs of leaks or water damage.

Air Conditioning and Electrical Systems: Evaluate the air conditioning units and water heaters to ensure they are of suitable model, capacity, and in proper working order. Inspect the electrical panel to confirm it is not outdated, is accessible, and functions correctly. Proper wiring is critical to prevent potential fire hazards. Check for sufficient and well-maintained power outlets.

Plumbing and Water Systems: Examine the pipes and fixtures. Turn on taps to test for proper function and adequate water pressure. It's essential to ensure that the plumbing is modern and that pipes are not made of lead, which would necessitate replacement. Also, evaluate the condition and age of the water heater.

Exterior and Maintenance: Outside the house, look for any signs of improper water drainage around the foundation. The ground should slope away from the foundation to prevent water accumulation. Inspect any porches to ensure they have proper foundation and not just set on soil. Evaluate the condition of driveways and walkways for cracks or damage. Observe the *landscaping to gauge overall maintenance;* it should be neat and well-kept. If there's a sprinkler system, check that it is functioning correctly. Additionally, if the home has a deck, look for signs of wear such as decay or termite damage.

Property History

Knowing the sales history of the property you're considering is crucial. Don't just rely on the summary provided in the listing; ask your agent for a more comprehensive background. Find out how long the property has been on the market, if it has been listed and withdrawn before, or if it has been relisted at a lower price. Understanding these details can help you gauge how much to offer.

You'll also need in-depth details from the property title, which includes the owner's name(s), the home's original construction date, mortgage history, parcel volume and folio number, and previous sales records. Information on property taxes. Make sure to conduct this search—it provides valuable insights into the property and could potentially save you money. This information can typically be obtained through your agent. If you are not working with an agent, you can access title information from the National Land Agency (NLA) and tax details from Tax Administration Jamaica.

Making the Choice

After you've gathered all the necessary information—viewed the house, inspected its condition, and reviewed public records—it's time to make your decision. Take a moment to step back and evaluate all the data at your disposal before deciding whether to purchase the house. This thoughtful approach ensures that you make an informed decision based on comprehensive research.

Keep in mind:

- You may need to make some compromises on your priorities. No home is completely perfect, and a first home is often considered a "starter" home on the path to your dream home. Even if it fits your needs, desires, and lifestyle well, there will be aspects you wish were different. You might wish the home were closer to a lovely park or in a more upscale neighborhood. Ultimately, you need to decide what factors are most important to you. If the neighborhood trumps the specific house, you might opt to look for a different type of property within the same area, such as an apartment instead of a townhouse.

- If finances are a concern, consider discussing with your bank the possibility of increasing your mortgage. However, proceed with caution and ensure it's something you can afford. Overextending financially just to secure a specific property isn't wise when there might be other, more affordable options available.

- Lower your expectations regarding the condition of the home. If your inspection revealed minor issues, you could still consider buying the property and addressing the repairs yourself. Use these issues as leverage to negotiate a lower price, obtaining repair cost estimates from professionals rather than relying on your own judgment or the seller's assessment.

- Be ready to walk away. This is crucial, especially if you find the required compromises are too significant. It's important not to become emotionally attached until the deal is finalized and you've moved in.

Remember, the path to homeownership is just beginning; it can also start with choosing land and building your own home. If this is the route you're considering, my book, " The ABC of Block & Steel Construction: Building Your Jamaican Home," will be an invaluable resource. It guides you through each step of the building process, ensuring not just a successful build but a rewarding experience.

CHAPTER 7

Buying a House: Key Strategies for Negotiating

After attending numerous open houses, meeting with builders, and scouring neighborhoods for the best deals, you've finally found a property that feels like "home," and you're ready to make an offer. Or perhaps you fell in love with a home right away and are keen to seal the deal quickly. Either way, congratulations! You've reached a critical and often challenging stage in the home-buying process: negotiating the price.

Begin by having a clear understanding of your financial situation and the financing options available to you. If you're a first-time buyer, remember that there are specific programs and loans designed to assist with down payments and mortgage rates, as discussed in earlier chapters. Knowing exactly how much you're prepared to spend will provide you with leverage and flexibility during negotiations.

Making Your First Offer Your Best Offer:

When it comes time to make your first offer on a home, thorough preparation and a strategic approach are essential. This step involves more than just responding to the listing price; it's about carefully considering the value of the property based on your own research and analysis.

A critical tool in this process is the Comparative Market Analysis (CMA), or COMPS, which your real estate agent can provide. This analysis helps you understand the property's market value relative to similar properties. From there, adjust your offer based on factors that may increase or decrease the property's value. For instance, if the current owners have recently upgraded the plumbing, this might increase the property's value. Conversely, if the plumbing is outdated and likely to need repairs soon, this should be factored into your offer. It's wise to get estimates for any significant repairs that are immediately necessary.

Stay informed about local market trends as well. Understand whether the market is rising or declining, and consider the volume of sales and new constructions in the area, which might influence home prices. While these analyses require time and effort, they will equip you with various options to consider. This is where the expertise of your real estate agent becomes invaluable. An experienced agent can efficiently assess all factors and help formulate a compelling initial offer.

Once you and your agent settle on an offer, it will be forwarded to the seller or their agent. The response could be an acceptance, a counteroffer, or a negotiation that could go back and forth until both parties reach an agreement. Following a successful negotiation, the home purchase will proceed to the "under contract" phase.

Negotiating the Purchase Price:

The aim of your negotiation should be to secure the house for an amount you're comfortable with, and if possible, even less than what you were prepared to pay. Establish the maximum amount you can afford and stick to it. Offering more than this maximum means you're stretching beyond your budget right from the start.

Your negotiation strategy will largely depend on the current market conditions. In a buyer's market, where there are more homes for sale than there are buyers, you'll find you have more room to maneuver. You might consider making an offer below the asking price, request home improvements, more favorable closing terms, or even ask the seller to cover some of the closing costs.

Conversely, in a seller's market—where there are more buyers than available homes—your bargaining power diminishes. Here, you might need to meet the seller's asking price quickly or risk losing out to another buyer Understanding the seller's motivation can also provide a negotiation advantage. Are they relocating for a job or looking to move quickly? If they're motivated sellers, they might be more open to negotiation to ensure a swift sale. If their home has been on the market for a long time or has seen multiple listings at the same price, this might indicate that the sellers are not in a hurry and could be holding out for a higher offer.

Remember, the ultimate goal for both parties is to conclude a sale. While it's easy to get caught up in the negotiation, keep your focus on achieving a fair deal. Stay realistic about what you can achieve given the market conditions and the seller's circumstances.

To maintain your focus during negotiations, employ the following strategies:

Utilize your real estate agent as a "middleman" to handle negotiations with the seller's agent. This approach not only saves time and reduces stress but can also unearth insights about the seller's intentions that might not be directly shared with you. Stay inquisitive; asking pointed questions can reveal crucial information about why the house is being sold, potentially giving you an edge in negotiations. Be prepared to compromise and make concessions during the process. And always keep your primary objective in mind: acquiring the house. Avoid getting bogged down by minor details early in the negotiations. It's often more effective to secure agreement on the major elements first before delving into the finer points.

Navigating Multiple Offers in a Seller's Market:

In a seller's market, it's common to face competition when bidding on a home. Sellers often weigh multiple offers simultaneously and will likely favor the most attractive one. They may choose to negotiate exclusively with one potential buyer, typically through a series of counteroffers.

As a buyer in a competitive market, it's crucial to make your offer stand out. One effective way to demonstrate serious intent is by getting preapproved for a mortgage, which reassures the seller of your financial credibility. Showcasing your ability to make a substantial down payment, can also strengthen your offer. Additionally, offering favorable mortgage terms or participating in financing programs that appeal to sellers can make your bid more attractive.

In markets where demand outstrips supply, offering the listing price—or even exceeding it—can be a strategic move. For example, in my own experience with clients, we offered $5.5 million on a property listed at $4.5 million, clearly signaling my client's serious interest and boosting our chances in a competitive environment. In addition, minimizing contingencies in your offer can also make it more appealing to a seller. A cleaner offer with fewer conditions is often more attractive and can expedite the buying process.

Negotiating and making an offer on a home involves careful preparation and strategic thinking, especially in competitive markets. Begin by understanding your financial position and securing pre-approval for a mortgage to demonstrate to sellers that you are a serious buyer. Comparative Market Analysis (CMA) can help you make an informed offer based on the value of similar properties in the area.

Navigating in a Buyer's Market:

When making an offer, also consider the market conditions. In a buyer's market, you have more leeway to negotiate and include conditions such as home improvements or closing cost contributions. In a seller's market, your ability to negotiate is lessened, and you may need to meet or exceed the asking price to stand out.

Effective tactics during negotiation include using your real estate agent as a buffer to handle discussions, being inquisitive about the seller's reasons for selling which could provide leverage, and being willing to compromise on certain points. Focus on the main goal of purchasing the home and avoid getting sidetracked by minor details.

If facing multiple offers, enhance your position by being financially prepared, possibly offering above the asking price, and reducing the number of contingencies in your offer. This approach signals to the seller that you are committed and ready to proceed quickly, increasing your chances of success in acquiring the property.

HOW TO AVOID MISTAKES DURING NEGOTIATIONS

Whether you're buying a house for the first time or just got carried away in the negotiation intensity, mistakes happen. Keep these simple rules in mind:

- *Be nice*. No one likes rude people. Try not to offend your seller during a house visit. For example, discussing necessary renovations and poor taste of the decorations may hurt feelings, if not the entire deal.

- *Be calm*. Don't express too much of an interest! Most of the specialists agree that when sellers see how much you want this house to become yours, they won't accept your first offer. To avoid a counteroffer, you should always play it cool, no matter how perfect this property is for you.

- *Think like a seller*. Change your perspective. Take a different look at this situation. Imagine you meet this house in 2, 5, or 10 years. Will it be possible, or does it lack some basic features that the housing markets consider essential?

- *Don't expect the price to lower after valuation*. Bid lower than you can pay, and make your final offer with the most comfortable price you can afford.

- *Sign cautiously*. Make sure you acknowledge all terms and realize all liabilities before you sign any documents. Once you sign the contract, there's no way to make amendments without renegotiating and signing a new one.

CHAPTER 8

What to Know About Home Inspections

The house hunt is over, and you decide to start the closing process on a For Sale By Owner house, which will soon-to-be home. You have visited the house and seen it at its best—beautifully polished, shiny, and welcoming. What if this is just part of the picture and something is hidden underneath its glossy surface? Issues here may vary, from termites and mold to leaking pipes or cracked support walls.

This is why, before closing a deal on your highly anticipated new property, you need to order a home inspection to be conducted. It will help to evaluate the house's condition and let you sleep safely at night before and after the purchase.

WHY DO YOU NEED A HOME INSPECTION?

Some buyers tend to skip this step, especially if the market is hot and you're competing with several other buyers. Home inspections cost money and take time; however, if there are serious issues found, more time and money is saved after a fair deal is closed. You need a house inspection to know what, exactly, you're buying and what to expect from your property in the future. Home Inspections are especially necessary when buying an older house.

During this process, specialists will examine the house to determine its condition and the viability of all the house systems. Don't confuse the home inspection with house appraisal. The inspection will clarify the current state of the house, not what it's actually worth. After the inspections, you'll receive a report on the state of the house. The report will contain suggestions for maintenance or repair steps or the need for additional expert opinions—for example, a structural engineer, should the inspection disclose faults in the building structure.

INSPECTIONS, INSPECTORS, AND COMMON MISTAKES

When inspecting a home, it's crucial to thoroughly examine various components to ensure everything is in good condition: There are different types of house inspections available. General or residential inspections will observe and give an evaluation of the house elements and systems. The list below contains points that can be enhanced or some of the points excluded. Nevertheless, here's an idea of what should/will be examined in a comprehensive residential inspection:

The exterior of the house, including water drainage systems and the overall state of the yard, trees, pathways, fences, decks, and stairs, should be evaluated for both functionality and aesthetic issues. The structural integrity of the home is equally important. Check the construction type, foundation, beams, columns, and the condition of walls to ensure everything is structurally sound and upright.

The roof requires special attention to assess the installation quality, any visible damage, and the condition of tiles, shingles, zinc, and gutters. Plumbing is another critical area; inspect for leaks, test water pressure, examine faucets, showers, and the material and age of pipes. Ensure the hot water system and septic tank, if present, are functioning properly.

Electrical systems must be up to code; check the electric box, fuses, and visible wiring for safety concerns. Also, evaluate the age and condition of any solar systems and air conditioning units to ensure they are operating effectively.

In the laundry room, look for proper ventilation, dryer systems functionality, and check for any leaks or potential fire hazards.

Bathrooms should be scrutinized for the condition of bathtubs, showers, sinks, and toilets, as well as for proper ventilation and plumbing functionality. Kitchen inspections should focus on the plumbing and cabinets to ensure they are in good working order and free from termites.

Fire safety is paramount; ensure that smoke detectors are installed and functioning. Lastly, a comprehensive pest inspection should be conducted to check for the presence of wood-boring insects, molds, and fungi, which can cause significant damage and health issues if not addressed.

If you live in certain high-risk areas, it's wise to order an additional service—for example, earthquake, hurricane or flood inspection. The specialist will help you to estimate the resistance of the property during natural disasters. Your inspector may recommend you ask for a specialized opinion, such as a structural engineer in case weakness is suspected in bearing walls.

A good expert is hard to find. Choosing the right inspector is the key to a thorough and comprehensive report. You may search online, paying attention to reviews of that inspector. Many real estate companies and lenders have a list of professionals. Ask your friends and family for a recommendation. An excellent source of recommendations is the real estate agent with whom you're working—your buyer's agent, not the seller's agent.

Common Mistakes:

Attending the home inspection is a critical step in the home-buying process that some buyers overlook. Rather than just reviewing the inspection report, being present allows you to tour the house with an expert and understand its condition and features firsthand. It's also an excellent opportunity to ask questions. Inspectors have a wealth of knowledge, and what might be common knowledge to them could be unfamiliar to you. Never hesitate to request clarification on anything you don't understand during the inspection.

A common oversight during inspections is not checking the utilities, especially if they are turned off. Buyers should request that utilities be activated to test for leaks and ensure everything is correctly connected. This is crucial for spotting potential issues that might not be apparent when systems are inactive.

For new constructions, the process slightly differs. Developers typically provide a new inspection report and offer a six months defects grace period. It's important to remember that new houses can have problems too, and all standard house inspection checks should be applied to newly built homes to ensure their quality and safety.

After the home inspection, you'll face one of three outcomes:

1. Ideal Outcome: The inspection reveals that the house is in excellent condition with no need for repairs. This allows you to proceed smoothly with the rest of the purchasing process.

2. Common Scenario: More often, the inspection might highlight the need for minor repairs. This could lead to negotiations for the repairs to be completed before moving forward, or you might negotiate a price reduction to cover the costs of these repairs yourself.

3. Worst-Case Scenario: In some cases, the inspection may uncover significant issues, such as a roof nearing the end of its lifespan or foundational problems that are costly to fix. In this situation, you might negotiate a significant reduction in the sale price to accommodate the cost of major repairs, or you may decide to walk away from the

purchase altogether. If the sale includes contingencies based on the home inspection, and the property fails this inspection, any deposit or earnest money you've paid should be refundable.

Regrettably, there isn't a one-size-fits-all approach for handling issues discovered during a home inspection, as much depends on the specific conditions set out in your purchase agreement. In an ideal situation, especially in a buyer's market, the seller might be responsible for all repairs. However, some agreements might set limits on liability or require costs to be split between buyer and seller. If you've agreed to buy the house "as is," similar to the situation with the "raining apartment," the inspection serves purely for your information, and you'll need to assess and budget for the necessary repairs after purchase.

Common issues to consider include the need for roof repairs or replacement, updating old plumbing, addressing any leaks, and potentially rewiring, especially in homes that are 30 to 50 years old.

WHEN TO WALK AWAY

Professionals say you should cancel the deal if you can't buy the house you want on the conditions that you want and for the money that you have. In a buyer's market, the seller will negotiate minor repairs disclosed by an inspection long before the thought to walk away hits you. However, some repairs are just not worth it. If the problem that the homeowner refuses to fix or pay for is dangerous and you can fix it, then it may be time to walk away. If the problem is something you need to fix soon, but it is too expensive for you, walk away. If the issue is likely to cause a chain of other problems, and it is hard to estimate how much it will cost, walk away.

Consider the pros and cons carefully, and listen to your real estate team's advice. They are usually more experienced and may explain to you the advantages and disadvantages better than anyone else. Also, listen to your own gut. If the doubts and uncertainties are too anxiety-provoking, it might be better to turn it down and start over.

Can inspections affect house value?

Yes, they can, although it's not common for an inspection to significantly alter the sale price once it's been negotiated. Viewing the inspection phase as an opportunity to renegotiate the price usually isn't effective. The primary purpose of a home inspection is to protect the buyer from unforeseen major issues that could accompany the purchase.

Conversely, a home appraisal evaluates the property's value to ensure that the lender does not finance more than the property is worth. Appraisals consider factors such as square footage, the number of rooms and bathrooms, the size of the property, and the presence of a garage. Appraisers use analytical data, including home features and comparable sales in the area, to determine the market price, incorporating these elements into complex mathematical evaluations.

While appraisals assess the home's market value based on visible conditions and comparisons, inspections focus on the physical condition of the home. Conditions like a moldy basement or a tiled facade are noticeable and factored into the appraisal. However, issues like electrical systems that don't meet code or foundational problems, which are not immediately apparent, typically don't affect the appraisal value.

When obtaining a mortgage, lenders may require a house inspection to ensure there are no significant issues, such as structural damage or faulty plumbing. This inspection is not about appraising the home's value but confirming its condition is satisfactory. A thorough and competent inspector is crucial for this process; they will scrutinize the home and identify any necessary repairs. Since the sale can hinge on the inspector's findings, choosing a highly skilled and reliable inspector is essential for a prospective buyer.

CHAPTER 9

Shopping for A Home Loan

Navigating the process of shopping for a home loan in Jamaica is a critical step in buying a home and requires meticulous planning, research, and comparison to ensure you secure the best deal that suits your financial situation. This guide aims to streamline your journey by providing a structured approach to finding the right mortgage and effectively navigating the complexities of loan shopping.

Despite the thorough preparation, every time I face the task of securing a mortgage to finalize a purchase, I'm gripped by a familiar anxiety. This fear stems from the numerous rejections I encountered during my first attempt to buy a home. Recently, while writing this book, I discovered a small plot of land with a rundown building that piqued my interest. Its prime location along a main thoroughfare presents immense potential, despite its asking price of 12 million. Yet, the thought of financing this project brings back all my old fears. Questions swirl in my mind: Can I secure a loan for this property? Should I leverage the equity from my other properties? Am I risking financial overextension, or worse, bankruptcy? Or should I consider forming a strategic partnership, or simply walk away? The multitude of options and the weight of the decision loom large, making it difficult to choose the best path forward.

Every time I face the challenge, I tackle it head-on, pushing through the initial uncertainty. Fueled by determination, I meticulously gather the required documents and move forward with confidence, drawing on the strength of past successes and the invaluable lessons I've learned along the way. Fear will not hold me back, and it shouldn't hold you back either, which is why being well-prepared is crucial. Every step taken and every document prepared represents a move away from the doubts that once overshadowed my ambitions. Inspired by Aunt Dolly's enduring resilience and the wisdom she imparted, I muster my resolve and proceed with the same determination I used to gather my school books, unwavering in the face of past rejections.

Understanding Your Financial Health

Your credit history is a key factor in determining the interest rates you receive. In Jamaica, you can obtain one free credit report each year from CRIF Information Bureau, and you can purchase a detailed report for a nominal fee. Improving your credit score can significantly influence the terms of your loan.

The debt-to-income ratio (DTI) is a crucial financial metric that measures the ratio of your monthly debt payments to your gross monthly income. For example, if you earn $20,000 a month before taxes and deductions and your monthly debt payments amount to $6000, your DTI would be calculated by dividing your total monthly debt by your monthly income. In this case, $6000 divided by $20,000 equals 0.3, or 30%, indicating that 30% of your monthly income is used to cover debt payments.

———————————

Lenders use the debt-to-income (DTI) ratio to evaluate whether a borrower can manage monthly debt payments and repay loans. A lower DTI ratio, which indicates a good balance between debt and income, suggests that the borrower poses a lower financial risk. On the other hand, a high DTI ratio, where a significant portion of income is devoted to debt repayment, could make it harder to secure additional credit or loans. Most lenders prefer a DTI ratio of 35 to 40% or lower, with no more than 30% dedicated to mortgage or rent payments.

Saving for a substantial down payment can also positively impact your loan terms. A larger down payment can lower your loan's interest rate and may help avoid the need for private mortgage insurance (PMI), ultimately improving the conditions of your loan.

Preparing for a Mortgage

When preparing for a mortgage, understanding the difference between pre-approval and pre-qualification is crucial. Opting for pre-approval gives you a more accurate estimate of how much you can borrow and enhances your credibility with sellers, making your offers more attractive.

Exploring Loan Options

In Jamaica, prospective homeowners have several loan options to consider:

Traditional Mortgages are available through banks and credit unions. These mortgages come with either fixed or variable interest rates and offer various term lengths to suit different financial situations.

National Housing Trust (NHT) Loans provide financing to contributors at subsidized interest rates, which are often more favorable than those offered by commercial banks. This makes NHT loans a popular choice for many Jamaicans.

Building Societies Loans are offered by institutions that specialize in mortgage lending, featuring competitive rates and terms tailored to meet diverse borrower needs.

Joint Finance Mortgages combine loans from the NHT and either a commercial bank or building society. This arrangement allows borrowers to finance more expensive properties than they could typically afford on a single income.

Vendor's Mortgage involves direct financing from the property seller, which can come with negotiated terms potentially beneficial to the buyer, such as lower interest rates or flexible repayment schedules.

Understanding these options will help you make an informed decision when choosing the best mortgage to finance your home purchase.

Choosing the Right Lender

When selecting a lender for your home loan, it's important to consider both the interest rates and the annual percentage rate (APR). Comparing APRs provides a comprehensive analysis of the total cost of the loan, including interest rates and other fees. This helps ensure you're getting the best deal possible.

The reputation of a lender is also crucial. Look into their customer service reviews and seek personal recommendations to ensure you choose a reliable lender known for fair dealing and good service. Additionally, be diligent about uncovering all associated costs with your loan. Investigate origination fees, closing costs, and any hidden fees to fully understand what you will be expected to pay. This upfront effort can help you avoid unexpected financial burdens later.

Finalizing Your Mortgage

Negotiating Loan Terms

When securing a home loan, don't hesitate to negotiate the terms. This can include seeking lower interest rates or requesting waivers for certain fees, which can significantly affect the total cost of your loan over time.

It's also crucial to thoroughly understand all the terms outlined in your loan agreement. Make sure you are clear about any penalties, special conditions such as prepayment penalties, or options for interest-only payments. Understanding these details upfront can help avoid surprises later.

Lastly, plan for the long-term affordability of your loan. Consider not just your current financial situation but also future potential changes in income and expenses. Ensuring that you can comfortably manage the loan payments throughout the term of the mortgage will help secure your financial stability.

Additional Considerations for Home Loans

When seeking a mortgage, it's beneficial to consult with mortgage brokers. They can offer a wide array of options and provide impartial advice, which is particularly valuable compared to the more limited and proprietary offerings from banks.

It's important to conduct a comprehensive comparison of mortgage rates. Don't just look at the interest rates; consider all associated fees as well. Remember that loans marketed as "no-fee" often incorporate these fees into the interest rates, which might not always be apparent.

Accuracy in your credit report is crucial for securing favorable loan terms. Obtain your credit report early in the process to correct any potential errors. This ensures you're in the best possible position to negotiate your mortgage.

Beyond the mortgage, remember to budget for the full cost of homeownership. This includes property taxes, homeowner's insurance, and ongoing maintenance costs—all of which contribute to the total cost of owning a home.

Finally, purchasing a home is more than just buying property; it's an investment in the surrounding community. Consider how your potential new home will impact your lifestyle, factoring in commute times, the quality of local schools, and available neighborhood amenities. These elements are essential to ensuring your new environment meets your long-term lifestyle needs.

Buyers should take an active role in the home purchasing process. Real estate agents work hard to negotiate the best deals, but your involvement is essential to ensure all aspects of the deal meet your needs as mortgage rates can fluctuate rapidly due to financial and market dynamics, which can be confusing and make timing crucial. For example, interest rates might be 5% one day and jump to 6% the next.

Furthermore, many homebuyers tend to consult only one lender, which can result in acquiring their "dream" home at a significantly higher monthly cost than if they had explored more financing options. Engaging in comprehensive research and comparison shopping among various lenders can lead to more favorable mortgage terms and ensure financial sustainability in your home purchase.

CHAPTER 10

Insurance, Property Valuation, and Property Survey

Purchasing a home involves navigating a series of challenges, especially for those unfamiliar with the intricacies of property transactions, ownership transfer, and financing. This guide aims to simplify these complexities by providing a straightforward roadmap through insurance requirements, property valuation, surveys, closing costs, and the details of your mortgage. Additionally, it includes a section called "10 Things to Know if You're Closing a Home Deal for the First Time." This resource offers essential tips to aid first-time homebuyers in managing the buying process effectively, ensuring they can handle potential challenges without them becoming overwhelming.

HOMEOWNER'S INSURANCE

When using a lender to finance your home purchase, you will need to secure homeowner's insurance prior to closing. Until the sale closes and the title transfers, it remains the seller's responsibility to maintain proper insurance coverage on the property. However, once the sale is finalized and ownership transfers, the seller's insurance coverage ends, and you, as the new owner, must have your own homeowner's insurance in place.

Lenders typically require proof that you have prepaid for one year of insurance coverage before they will release the funds for the purchase. Some lenders may offer the option to advance the payment for the insurance premium and include it in your monthly mortgage payments. This is because the lender, holding a lien on the property until the mortgage is fully paid, needs to ensure financial protection against potential damages to the house, ensuring they can recover the cost of rebuilding if necessary.

A typical homeowner's insurance policy provides coverage for a variety of risks including:

- Fire and lightning damage

- Hurricane-related damage

- Theft and vandalism incidents

- Damage from smoke

- Damage from falling objects such as tree limbs

- Damage caused by vehicles or aircraft impacting your property

- Riot or civil commotion damage

- Explosions

Homeowner's insurance typically covers liability, personal belongings, structures on your property such as sheds and fences, and additional living expenses if you cannot live in your home temporarily due to damage.

There are advantages to paying your homeowner's insurance premium upfront at closing. Doing so allows you to exclude this expense from your closing costs, which are usually paid all at once and include lender fees and your down payment.

Alternatively, you can choose to roll the cost of your insurance into your monthly mortgage payments. This option might be influenced by your mortgage agreement. Some lenders also set up an escrow account to help manage large homeownership costs like your mortgage, property taxes, and homeowner's insurance. This breaks the expenses into manageable monthly payments. The lender manages this account, which simplifies your financial commitments by ensuring these significant expenses are paid on time without direct intervention from you.

LIFE INSURANCE

Securing life insurance when taking out a mortgage is essential for both security and peace of mind.

Financial Security for Your Family: If you were to pass away before the mortgage is paid off, life insurance helps ensure that your family won't have to shoulder the remaining mortgage debt. It acts as a financial safety net, allowing your family to retain ownership of the home without financial strain.

Peace of Mind:Having life insurance means knowing that your family will be financially protected and can maintain their living standards, even in your absence. This assurance can provide significant peace of mind, knowing that your mortgage responsibilities will be covered.

Life insurance plays a crucial role in securing the financial stability of a family, especially when paired with homeownership. It ensures that in the event of the untimely death of the primary earner, the family can remain in their home, safeguarding them from the need to relocate or face foreclosure. This stability is vital for maintaining the household's standard of living. Additionally, obtaining life insurance at a younger age can capitalize on lower premiums, making it an economical choice for long-term financial security. By covering mortgage payments during unforeseen events, life insurance provides a critical safety net, preserving both the family's home and their financial future.

PROPERTY VALUATION

During the closing process of a real estate transaction, a crucial step involves the valuation and survey of the property by a licensed real estate appraiser. This expert determines the market value of the property to ensure that neither the buyer nor the mortgage lender is entering into a financially disadvantageous agreement due to an overestimated property value.

Appraisers and inspectors serve different functions. While an appraiser assesses the property to identify any obvious issues that might affect its value, an inspector conducts a more thorough check of the home's details, such as plumbing and electrical systems. The appraisal is essential for the bank's loan approval process and the cost of this service is typically covered by the buyer.

In evaluating a property, an appraiser may use one of two main methods. The sale comparison approach involves comparing the property with similar ones recently sold in the area to determine its value. Alternatively, the cost approach, which is often used for new constructions, estimates the cost to replace the building's structure. This comprehensive evaluation is intended to protect all parties involved by providing an accurate market value of the property.

PROPERTY SURVEY

A property survey provides detailed insight into the physical and legal aspects of a property, helping buyers make well-informed real estate investment decisions and avoid unexpected costs later. Property surveys are essential tools that provide crucial details about a property, helping buyers and lenders understand various aspects that could impact ownership and use

Boundary identification is one key feature of a property survey is , which precisely delineates the property's limits. This clarity is crucial for new owners, ensuring they understand the full extent of their land and helping to prevent future disputes with neighbors. Additionally, clear knowledge of property lines is indispensable for planning any construction, extensions, or landscaping projects on the property.

Easements and rights-of-way are significant features revealed in property surveys. These grant specific rights to others to use parts of the property for purposes such as utility access or shared driveways. Understanding these can help prevent future legal conflicts.

Zoning compliance information, showing how the property may be used under local regulations. This is vital for buyers to ensure that their intended use aligns with zoning laws, avoiding potential legal issues.

Identify any encroachments where the property or its structures might overstep onto neighboring lands or public areas. Identifying such issues early allows for resolutions before completing a purchase, either through direct negotiation with the seller or by planning for adjustments.

Finally, lenders often require a property survey during the mortgage approval process to confirm that the property is a suitable guarantee for the loan and free from severe encumbrances or title issues that could affect its value as collateral. This step is critical to securing financing and safeguarding the lender's investment.

Ultimately, conducting a property survey grants buyers peace of mind by providing a detailed overview of the property's physical characteristics, legal boundaries, and potential limitations or encumbrances. This thorough understanding helps buyers make informed decisions, ensuring that their real estate investment is sound and free from unforeseen complications that could prove costly in the future. Armed with the comprehensive insights from a property survey, buyers can confidently navigate the purchase process and plan for any necessary adjustments or negotiations.

CHAPTER 11

The Closing Costs

Here's a discussion of typical closing costs when buying a home in Jamaica:

Sale/Construction/Home Owners Agreements

Each of these agreements plays a crucial role in different stages of homeownership, whether it's purchasing a new or used property, constructing a new home, or living within a managed community. It's essential for all parties involved to carefully review and understand the terms of these agreements to ensure compliance and mitigate potential conflicts.

A Sale Agreement, also known as a purchase agreement or sales contract, is a legally binding document that outlines the terms and conditions of property sales between a buyer and a seller. This agreement typically includes details such as the property's description, purchase price, down payment, closing date, contingencies (such as financing or property survey), and any other terms agreed upon by both parties. Once signed by both the buyer and seller, the sales agreement serves as the foundation for the real estate transaction and guides the process until the closing.

A Construction Agreement is a contract between a property owner (client) and a construction company or contractor outlining the terms and conditions for a construction project. This agreement details the scope of work, project timeline, specifications, materials to be used, payment terms, warranties, and any other relevant provisions.

Construction agreements aim to ensure clarity and accountability throughout the construction process, protecting both parties' interests and minimizing disputes.

A Homeowners Association agreement, also known as CC&Rs (Covenants, Conditions, and Restrictions), outlines the rules, regulations, and obligations that homeowners within a specific community must adhere to. These agreements typically cover issues such as property maintenance standards, architectural guidelines, use of common areas, payment of HOA fees, and enforcement mechanisms for violations. Homeowners Association agreements aim to maintain the community's aesthetics, preserve property values, and facilitate harmonious living among residents.

Attorney fees usually charge the fees for the various agreements discussed above and in addition, cover services such as title searches, other document preparation, contract review, and overall legal guidance. Attorney fees can vary based on the complexity of the transaction and the lawyer's rates.

Valuation Fees Before finalizing the mortgage, lenders usually require a valuation of the property to determine its market value. Valuation fees cover the cost of hiring a professional appraiser to assess the property's worth. These fees are typically paid by the buyer and can vary depending on the property's size and location.

Property Survey Fees: Property surveys are required by lenders or buyers to confirm boundaries, easements, and other property details. Survey fees cover the cost of hiring a commissioned Land Surveyor to conduct the survey and prepare the necessary documentation. The buyer is typically responsible for paying survey fees.

Mortgage Fees:If obtaining a mortgage to finance the purchase, buyers may incur various mortgage-related fees. These fees can include loan application fees, appraisals, fees for mortgage insurance premiums, and other charges associated with securing the loan. Ask your bank for a breakdown of these fees and carefully review the terms of the mortgage agreement to understand all associated costs.

Government fees and charges are crucial considerations for buyers, encompassing stamp duty, transfer tax, registration fees, and land titling fees when applicable. It's important for buyers to fully understand these costs to ensure proper budgeting. Generally, the seller pays the transfer tax, which is calculated at 2% of the sale price. In Jamaica, the stamp duty is currently fixed at JMD $5,000. Additionally, registration fees are calculated at 0.25% of the sale price.

Home Owners Association (HOA) and Strata Housing

A Homeowners Association (HOA) and Strata Housing refer to organized communities that often come with the benefit of shared amenities and communal areas, such as swimming pools, fitness centers, security systems, and beautifully maintained landscapes. These communities typically require the payment of fees to fund their maintenance and improvement. and play a crucial role in maintaining and enhancing community living standards. Here's how these fees are typically utilized:

Maintenance of Common Areas: HOA fees help maintain parks, clubhouses, and community pools, ensuring these shared spaces are clean, functional, and enjoyable for all residents.

Landscaping: These fees support the regular landscaping of communal spaces, enhancing the overall aesthetics of the community and helping to maintain or increase property values.

Amenities: Fees often cover the costs associated with community amenities such as gyms, tennis courts, and playgrounds, ensuring they are well-maintained and regularly upgraded.

Infrastructure Maintenance: The fees contribute to the upkeep of essential infrastructure like roads, sidewalks, street lights, and benches, ensuring they remain in good condition.

Insurance and Reserve Funds: A portion of HOA fees is allocated towards insurance coverage for common areas and liability claims. Additionally, HOAs set aside funds for future large-scale projects or emergency repairs, providing a financial safety net for unforeseen circumstances.

Strata fees are essential for the upkeep and operation of community housing such as condominiums and townhouses. Here's how these fees are used:

Building Maintenance: Strata fees fund the maintenance of building exteriors and common indoor areas, ensuring the property remains in good condition and preserves its value.

Utility Costs: These fees often cover utilities for common areas, including water, sewage, and garbage disposal, ensuring these essential services are maintained for all residents.

Management Services: The fees provide for professional management services that handle the daily operations and governance of the strata community, helping everything run smoothly.

Bylaw Enforcement: Part of the fees goes towards enforcing community rules and regulations, which helps maintain order and stability within the community.

Contingency Funds: Like HOAs, strata communities allocate a portion of fees to contingency reserves. This fund is crucial for covering unexpected expenditures and ensuring the community is financially prepared for any emergencies.

In both HOA and Strata Housing communities, the collection of these fees is fundamental for sustaining the quality and value of the properties within. These fees ensure that residents enjoy well-maintained and secure living environments while protecting and potentially enhancing the value of their investments. Homeowners are encouraged to actively participate in their HOA or strata meetings to understand and have a say in how these fees are managed.

SUMMARY

Buying a home is an exciting milestone, but it's also a process that requires careful planning and attention to detail. This guide takes you through each step of the journey, helping you make informed decisions as you move toward owning your dream home.

The first step in the home-buying process is to define your budget. It's important to evaluate how much you have saved for a down payment and consider what your monthly mortgage payments will look like. Additionally, you'll need to account for other costs, such as property taxes, homeowners insurance, and maintenance expenses, to ensure that your home purchase fits comfortably within your financial situation.

Once you've determined your budget, the next step is to get pre-approved for a mortgage. A mortgage pre-approval will give you a clear understanding of how much you can borrow, and it shows sellers that you are a serious buyer with the financial backing needed to complete the purchase. Pre-approval also puts you in a stronger position when making an offer on a home.

With your budget and mortgage pre-approval in place, it's time to find a real estate agent. A knowledgeable agent is a valuable asset in your home-buying journey. They will guide you through the market, help you find properties that meet your needs, negotiate offers, and manage the paperwork. Their expertise is critical when it comes to navigating the complexities of the local market and ensuring that you are making a sound investment.

Now comes the fun part—searching for your new home. With your real estate agent's assistance, you'll begin looking for properties that match your preferences and fit within your budget. This stage can take some time, as it's important to consider factors like location, size, style, and any must-have features. Whether you're looking for a starter home, a forever home, or an investment property, patience is key in finding the right fit.

When you've found a home you love, it's time to make an offer. Your agent will help you determine a fair and competitive price based on the market and guide you through the negotiation process. Offers often include contingencies, such as a home inspection or appraisal, to protect your interests as a buyer.

A home inspection is essential to ensure that the property is in good condition before you finalize the purchase. A professional inspector will evaluate the home for any potential issues, such as structural concerns, electrical or plumbing problems, or necessary repairs. If significant issues are discovered, you may renegotiate with the seller or request that they make repairs before closing.

Next, your lender will require a home appraisal. This step ensures that the property's market value aligns with the loan amount. The appraiser evaluates the home based on various factors, such as its condition, location, and recent sales of comparable homes. If the appraisal comes in lower than expected, it could lead to renegotiations with the seller or impact your loan approval.

Once the inspection and appraisal are completed, you can finalize your mortgage. This involves working with your lender to complete any remaining paperwork and locking in your interest rate. At this stage, you're getting closer to officially becoming a homeowner.

The final step is closing. At closing, you'll sign all the necessary legal documents, pay closing costs, and officially transfer ownership of the property. Once everything is signed and sealed, the home is yours, and you'll receive the keys to your new property.

Congratulations! You've successfully navigated the home-buying process, and it's time to move into your new home. With the right planning and guidance, you've achieved an important milestone, and now you can enjoy the space you've worked so hard to secure.

APPENDIX A

Step-by-Step Guide to Applying for a Mortgage

1. Assess Your Financial Health:Review your credit score, income, debts, and savings. Your financial health will significantly influence your loan eligibility and interest rates.

2. Choose the Right Type of Loan: Based on your financial assessment and the property you're interested in, decide which loan type best suits your needs.

3. Gather Necessary Documents: Prepare the required documentation, which typically includes identification, Tax Registration Number (TRN), proof of income (pay slips, Accountant Statement), employment verification letter, bank statements, Sales Agreement, Closing Cost statement (from seller's Lawyer), Survey Identification Report, and Valuation Report.

4. Submit Your Application: Approach your chosen lender or the NHT (see resources for additional requirements from the NHT) to submit your mortgage application along with all required documents.

5. Property Valuation and Inspection: The lender will require a professional valuation and possibly an inspection of the property to ensure it meets their lending criteria.

6. Wait for Approval: After submitting your application, there will be a waiting period during which the lender assesses your eligibility and the property details.

7. Closing the Deal: Once approved, you will proceed to closing, where you sign the mortgage agreement, and other legal documents, and finalize the sale.

Approaching the mortgage market with a thorough understanding of your options and a clear plan can significantly impact the success of your home purchase. By diligently researching, comparing, and negotiating, you can secure a mortgage that not only meets your current needs but also supports your long-term financial health.

APPENDIX B

9 THINGS TO KNOW IF YOU'RE CLOSING A HOME DEAL FOR THE FIRST TIME

1. Open a House Account

When gearing up to buy a new home, placing all your dedicated funds into one account emerges as a smart strategy. This approach simplifies the financial side of the home-buying journey, making it easier to manage and keep track of your money. Here's why this method is worth considering:

2. Negotiate the interest rate

Where possible shop around and negotiate the interest rate and bank fees being charged for the loan.

3. Have a Home Inspection

In older homes it is important to have a home inspection. Making sure nothing falls off on the first day in your new home or your water heater does not work is generally enough reason to have a home inspection. Engage specialists to check the air conditioning system, plumbing, and electricity. They will also check mold growth and other issues.

4. Have a Pest Inspection

The best approach is to hire a licensed pest inspection company. They'll check your future property for contamination by flies, mosquitoes, cockroaches, fleas, rats, mice, bedbugs, termites, ants, and other types of pests.

5. Fix All the Issues after the Inspections

If inspections revealed any problems, you may want to ask for a price adjustment to cover the cost of repair or ask the seller to fix the problems. Some inspectors are willing to look deeper into the issue. They say you should ask for a second opinion or evaluate it further with a specialist. It's highly recommended to discuss the estimates and fix the issues as soon as possible.

6. Title Search and Caveats

Buyers should ensure their legal representatives conduct Title search and check for liens caveats and encumbrances.

a. *Title.* In real estate, "title" refers to the legal ownership of a property. When you have the title to a property, you have the right to use, possess, and dispose of that property as you wish, subject to any legal restrictions or encumbrances. Title can be transferred from one party to another through a deed or other legal instrument.

b. *Liens.* Liens are legal claims or encumbrances on a property that serve as security for the payment of a debt or obligation. When a lien is placed on a property, it means that the property is used as collateral until the debt is paid off or the obligation is fulfilled. Common types of liens include mortgage liens (for home loans), tax liens (for unpaid taxes), and mechanic's liens (for unpaid construction work).

c. *Caveats.* Caveats are notices lodged against a property title to protect the interests of the person lodging the caveat. They serve as a warning to potential buyers or lenders that someone else has an interest in the property. Caveats are commonly used to prevent the registration of certain transactions, such as sales or mortgages, until the caveator's interest is resolved.

d. *Encumbrances*. Encumbrances are any claims, liens, mortgages, or other restrictions that affect the title to a property and may diminish its value or restrict its use. Encumbrances can include easements (rights to use another person's land for a specific purpose), restrictive covenants (agreements that limit how the property can be used), and leases (agreements giving someone else the right to use the property for a specific period). Essentially, encumbrances are anything that burdens the property's title.

7. Home Appraisal

A home appraisal determines the estimated market value of the property you plan to buy. The appraiser considers factors such as the overall condition of the home, its geographic location, proximity to key attractions, the value of nearby homes, recent sales, and the potential growth of the neighborhood. Mortgage lenders rely on this appraisal to ensure the loan amount aligns with the home's value.

If the appraisal comes in lower than the agreed price, the lender may not approve the loan for that amount. In such cases, the seller might lower the price, but not all sellers are willing to negotiate. Keep in mind that the appraised value is not binding—final negotiations between the buyer, seller, and lender determine the sale price, which can influence whether the deal moves forward or stalls.

8. Set the Time and Date of the Closing

The closing date is a negotiable factor during the offer and acceptance phase of a home sale transaction. When making an offer, the buyer will include a closing date and, depending on the seller's circumstances, it might be acceptable or could be, Don't choose a date casually. The right date can ensure a smooth closing and reduce closing costs; the wrong date puts the home buyer at risk of not closing on time, needlessly complicating the move, increasing expenses, and even losing your new home.

If you schedule a closing and fail to complete it on that day, there are consequences. You'll face increased closing costs the next month, in addition to any penalty for the delay. Although most sellers will work with you if the transaction does not close on time, failure to close opens the door to canceling the sale. This is more likely to occur in a seller's market, in which the seller may have backup offers that are potentially better than yours.

9. Be Present at a Walkthrough

A final walkthrough is a last chance to see your future house before you buy it. The property should be in the condition that's specified in your sales contract. You may inspect for any changes made subsequent to the home or pest inspections. Check if everything is in order and if any additional replacements are necessary.

APPENDIX C

Professionals

Here's a list of trusted professionals I've worked with to help my buyers and sellers achieve their real estate goals. I encourage you to explore their services through the links provided and consider them for your needs. Be sure to mention that I referred you when reaching out.

Claudia Davis - Realtor

Unit 8c Seymour Park 2 Seymour Avenue Kingston 6

sivad.claudia@gmail.com

876-292-6776

Toniann Dietrich - Realtor Associate

Unit 8c Seymour Park 2 Seymour Avenue Kingston 6

toni.dietrich@gmail.com

876 -370-8138

Tamaika Mills - Realtor Associate

Unit 8c Seymour Park 2 Seymour Avenue Kingston 6

tami.drealtor@gmail.com

876- 835-8323

Ericson Wilson - Realtor Associate

Unit 8c Seymour Park 2 Seymour Avenue Kingston 6

ericsonwilson@yahoo.com

876-470-8345

JN Bank Mortgage Officer - Yaneek Grant

Link: https://trfmz.com/cJotGQDPKLQf1DgoBPeI

VMBS Mortgage Officer - Charmaine McIntosh

Link: https://trfmz.com/JHcfYcoyYRGrPKiw

CIBC Caribbean Mortgage Officer - Romel Wilson

Link: https://zfrmz.com/IDFoUHTuzWxesPJaBwJa

NCB Mortgage Officer - Wendy Kelly

Link: https://trfmz.com/a1KnfGQTVRRvIMMITY

Architect - Damien Valentine

Link: https://trfmz.com/GdJMMvrQoYSyGeo7YbUc1

Draftsman - Carlton Wright

Link: https://trfmz.com/EF3yq3HoFpYJrmXki9xQT

Commissioned Land Surveyor - Elfeego Harris

Link: https://trfmz.com/DhNAXiwqJ2fz6nOVfgT

Don't miss out!

Visit the website below and you can sign up to receive emails whenever Claudia Davis publishes a new book. There's no charge and no obligation.

https://books2read.com/r/B-A-VCTOC-STSCF

BOOKS 2 READ

Connecting independent readers to independent writers.

About the Author

Since 2008, Claudia Davis has excelled in the real estate industry, consistently leading her teams to success as a top sales producer. Her deep knowledge of the Jamaican real estate market and commitment to her clients have earned her a reputation as a trusted advisor. She holds a BSc in Human Resource Management with First Class Honours from the University of Technology, Jamaica, and has earned certifications in Real Estate Sales, Dealers Courses, Construction Levels 1 and 2, and Paralegal studies.

Beyond her accomplishments, Claudia is passionate about empowering others to achieve financial independence through real estate. Guided by her motto, *"Be great to yourself, Buy Real Estate,"* her experience and expertise form the foundation of her book, *The Ultimate Guide to Homeownership in Jamaica,* aimed at inspiring the next generation—including her children and grandchildren—on their journey to financial success and homeownership.

Claudia Davis

sivad.claudia@gmail.com

Read more at https://claudiadavisja.com.